Charles Dwight Willard

The Free Harbor Contest at Los Angeles

Charles Dwight Willard

The Free Harbor Contest at Los Angeles

ISBN/EAN: 9783744676946

Printed in Europe, USA, Canada, Australia, Japan

Cover: Foto ©ninafisch / pixelio.de

More available books at **www.hansebooks.com**

THE

FREE HARBOR CONTEST

AT LOS ANGELES

AN ACCOUNT OF THE LONG FIGHT WAGED BY THE PEOPLE
OF SOUTHERN CALIFORNIA TO SECURE A HARBOR
LOCATED AT A POINT OPEN TO
COMPETITION

> "There is a tide in the affairs of men,
> Which, taken at the flood leads on to fortune;
> Omitted, all the voyage of their life
> is bound in shallows and in miseries."—Julius Caesar.

By CHARLES DWIGHT WILLARD

LOS ANGELES, CALIFORNIA
KINGSLEY-BARNES & NEUNER COMPANY, Publishers
JULY, 1899

THE AUTHOR DEDICATES THIS BOOK TO

JOHN F. FRANCIS,

NOT FROM ANY SENTIMENT OF PERSONAL REGARD, ALTHOUGH SUCH A SENTIMENT EXISTS, BUT BECAUSE HE IS AN ADMIRABLE REPRESENTATIVE OF THE TYPE OF MODERN AMERICAN CITIZENSHIP THAT UNDERSTANDS AND ACCEPTS ITS RESPONSIBILITIES TO THE GENERAL PUBLIC, AND THAT FINDS IN ITS INDIVIDUAL PROSPERITY SOMETHING ABOVE AND BEYOND THE MEANS FOR PLEASURE OR THE OPPORTUNITY FOR CONTINUED SELFISH GAIN.

CONTENTS.

CHAPTER I. NATURE OF THE CONTEST. River and harbor bills. Corporate influences. Prejudice against the Southern Pacific Railway in California. Effect of the contest on the city of Los Angeles.

CHAPTER II. WHY THE HARBOR WAS NEEDED. Opportunity for trans-Pacific Commerce. Oriental business at present. Advantages of a southwestern port. San Pedro a natural harbor.

CHAPTER III. THE ANCIENT PORT OF SAN PEDRO. Discovery and exploration. The Mission era. Dana's visit. Description of the harbor.

CHAPTER IV. WORK ON THE INTERIOR HARBOR. Possibilities for development. The first appropriation. Result of the work. The great boom of 1887. Birth of the deep-sea harbor idea.

CHAPTER V. ENTER THE CHAMBER OF COMMERCE. A unique organization. Scope of its work. Deep-sea agitation begins. Senator Frye visits the harbor. His singular attitude on the question.

CHAPTER VI. THE GOVERNMENT CONSIDERS THE OUTER HARBOR. The Board of 1890-1. It reports for San Pedro. Mr. Huntington succeeds Gov. Stanford to the presidency of the road.

CHAPTER VII. THE SOUTHERN PACIFIC'S CHANGE OF BASE. The early history of Santa Monica. Redondo as a port. The Terminal Railway. A question of local commerce.

CHAPTER VIII. THE ISSUE TAKES SHAPE. Senator Felton's effort for a deep-sea appropriation. The Hood telegram. Mr. T. E. Gibbon. A new Board is appointed to investigate.

CHAPTER IX. THE CRAIGHILL BOARD. A public session. Attitude of the Chamber of Commerce. Criticism of the Southern Pacific. The report of the Board for San Pedro.

CHAPTER X. A DECISION THAT DID NOT DECIDE. General Forman's mission to Washington. His report pleads for unity. W. H. Mills speaks for the railroad at the Redondo banquet. The issue is reopened. Work of the Los Angeles Times.

CHAPTER XI. THE CHAMBER OF COMMERCE TAKES A VOTE. Completion of the Long Wharf at Santa Monica. Mr. Huntington speaks. Mr. Crawley's resolution. Combat in the Chamber of Commerce. The members choose San Pedro.

CHAPTER XII. THE WINTER OF OUR DISCONTENT. White in the Senate. Mr. Huntington's strength. The Eastern newspapers take notice.

CHAPTER XIII. THE FREE HARBOR LEAGUE. A savage circular. The League is formed. Col. Benyaurd's project. The inner harbor idea.

CHAPTER XIV. THE TRAP IS SPRUNG. The League sends delegates to Washington. Mr. Hermann of Oregon arranges matters. He writes a letter.

CHAPTER XV. THE DOUBLE APPROPRIATION SCHEME. Mr. McLachlan's telegram. His peculiar position. The Chamber of Commerce on the rack.

CHAPTER XVI. THE STRUGGLE IN THE SENATE. Los Angeles delegations before the Committee on Commerce. The two reports. Senator White's amendment, His speech. Mr. Frye responds. The compromise.

CHAPTER XVII. ONE MORE FINAL DECISION. Reception to White and Perkins. The Walker Board appointed. Mr. Morgan. Sessions of the Board; its report.

CHAPTER XVIII. THE SECRETARY OF DELAY. Feeling against the railroad. Russel A. Alger, Secretary of War. His collection of excuses. The appropriation in the House. Mr. Cooper's speech.

CHAPTER XIX. THE JUBILEE AT SAN PEDRO. Ceremonies at the beginning of the work.

CHAPTER XX. THE PRESENT WORK. The contractors. Nature of the specifications. The inner and outer harbor. Efforts for further development.

ACKNOWLEDGMENT.

The writer finds himself under obligation to a number of people and organizations in the preparation of this book, for courtesies of various kinds, and he takes this means of expressing his gratitude: To the Land of Sunshine, the Capital, Terminal Railway, Chamber of Commerce, City Librarian Mrs. H. C. Wadleigh, Harry E. Brook, Captain J. J. Meyler, C. V. Barton, J. F. Francis, W. B. Cline, F. K. Rule, Terminal Land Co., Southern California Lumber Co., J. R. Newberry, H. Jevne, W. C. Patterson, F. W. Braun, L. W. Blinn, Kerckhoff-Cuzner Co., Cal Byrne, J. E. Plater, N. Blackstone, E. W. Jones, Bishop & Co., N. Bonfilio, J. Ross Clark, K. Cohn & Co., Los Angeles Farming and Milling Co., Maier & Zobelein, Boston Store, Coulter Dry Goods Co., Harris & Frank, Geo. S. Patton, T. E. Gibbon, J. D. Hooker, D. C. McGarvin, Will Knippenberg, Chas. Weir, W. D. Woolwine, Frank Wiggins, Harry E. Andrews, Harry Chandler.

THE TWO VIEWS.

Senator Berry of Arkansas in the San Pedro-Santa Monica Debate before the Senate, May 11th, 1899:

Take it all in all this is the most extraordinary proposition I have ever known to be submitted to the Congress of the United States.

I do not believe there is a man throughout the whole United States, save and except Mr. Huntington, who would have had the assurance, in the face of the reports of the army officers, to have come to the Congress of the United States, and asked them to give him $3,000,000 in money to build a breakwater to serve his private interests.

It is much better that no deep-water harbor should ever be had, better far that the money should be utterly and absolutely thrown to the winds, than that we should make thousands of people believe that the appropriation was made, not in the public interests, but in order to promote the private interests of individuals, be those individuals whom they may, whether the most powerful man in the land or the humblest citizen who walks this Union. In either case, if it be once understood that the Senate will be controlled by the reports of private engineers made for private individuals, then Mr. President, the River and Harbor Bill will no longer be considered for the best interests of the entire republic, but it will be solely a question as to who can bring the greatest influence to bear.

Senator Frye of Maine in the San Pedro-Santa Monica Debate before the Senate, May 12th, 1899.

Oh, it is too paltry to undertake to stop any legislation with that cheap demagogical cry that because Huntington has done it, no help can be given to Huntington. He employs today 75,000 men; pays them their wages when they are due, and there never has been a laboring man who has worked for him to whom he has not given his wages the day they were due. One instance I know where a railroad was a total wreck and owed the laborers $500,000, and Mr. Huntington put his hand into his pocket, gave the $500,000 to the railroad, wrecked as it was, took the wrecked road as security, and put his energy and courage into the railroad, and brought it up to life, activity and value. . . . Mr. Huntington is not bulling the stock markets, nor bearing them. He is not cornering wheat or flour. He is engaged in enormous enterprises, the results of which are building up the commerce of this republic, and in all his enterprises he is successful.

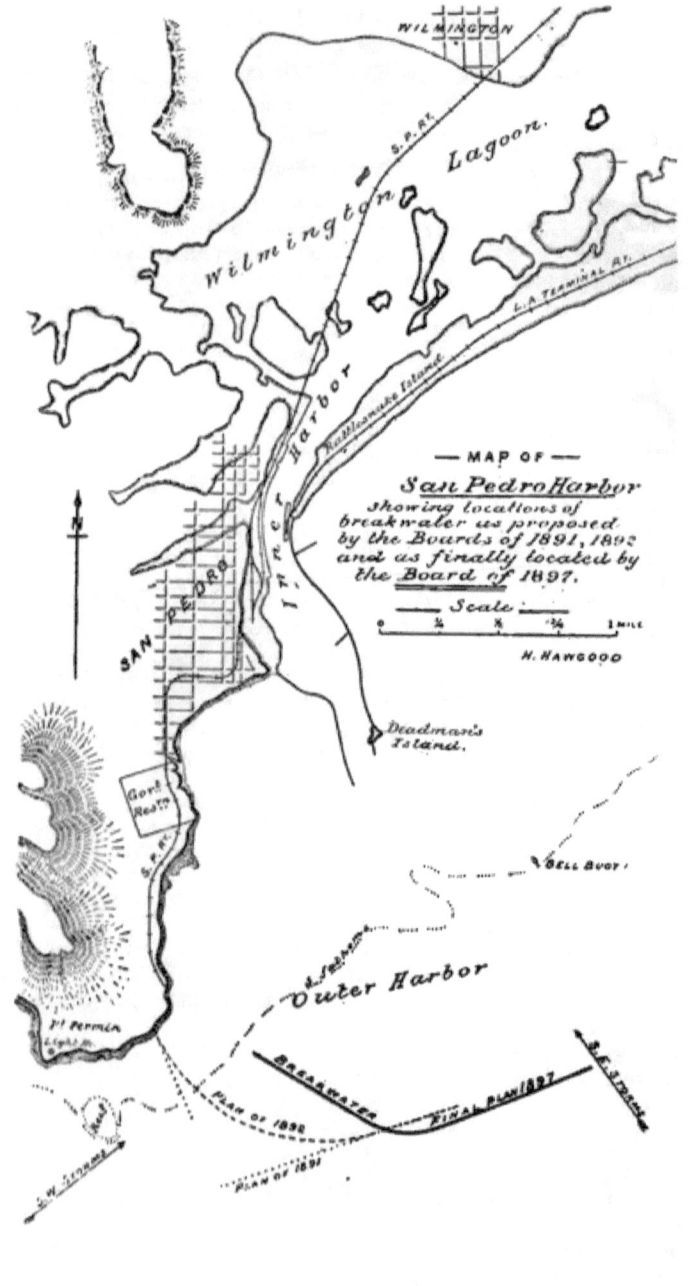

CHAPTER I.

The Nature of the Contest.

THE Congress of the United States passes every year a bill for the improvement of rivers and harbors, containing appropriations that vary in total from twelve to fifteen millions of dollars.

This is for expenditure direct. In addition to that, it adopts each year a number of projects for river and harbor improvement, for which sums amounting to an average of over seven millions a year are subsequently paid out through a general appropriation bill.*

The measure which is technically known as the "River and Harbor Bill" originates in the House of Representatives in the committee of that name. After it has been acted upon by the House, it goes up to the Senate, where it is considered first by the Committee on Commerce—for the upper chamber has no River and Harbor committee—and then by the whole Senate. If amendments are made by the Senate—which usually happens—the bill is likely to pass through the hands of a Conference Committee, made up of members from both houses, before it is finally adopted and becomes a law.

The process of legislation by Congress is long and tedious enough, even if the measure under consideration is generally acceptable and free from complication; but the River and Harbor bill, which is a vast composite of special and individual interests, extends as a rule from one end of the ses-

---

*For example, the bill of 1896, of which the San Pedro project formed part, contained $11,452,115 of direct appropriation, i. e. money to be paid without further action by Congress, on definitely specified work. It also contained projects which, according to the estimates of the engineers, might call for a total of $60,623,871.91. These projects would presently be submitted to contractors, and bids taken on them. As a rule, the bids would be under the specified sums: sometimes, as in the case of San Pedro, requiring less than 50 per cent. The total amount needed for the project being thus established, it is thereafter appropriated in parts, not exceeding 25 per cent of the total per annum, in the Sundry Civil Appropriation bill.

sion to the other, and permeates, with doubtful influence, the whole course of the legislation by which it is surrounded.

The customary off-hand opinion of the American voter with reference to the River and Harbor bill is that it is principally made up of big steals—that it represents a systematic and organized pilfering of the government by railroads, steamship companies, contractors and promoters, aided and abetted by the various communities which the improvements would advantage. Such a taint will of necessity attach to all measures that directly affect the business interests of individuals, and it is only through the exercise of the utmost discretion by the authorities of the government, both in the system under which the work is done and in the selection of desirable projects, that actual scandal is avoided.*

That it is not always avoided, the extraordinary experience of the people of Los Angeles, in their effort to secure a harbor not under corporate control—an experience which is to be set forth in detail in this narration—will show.

The difficulties that surround the government in its work of river and harbor improvement are greatly enhanced by a lack of discrimination and too often by a moral obtuseness on the part of the communities whose interests are involved. It is precisely because the case of Los Angeles, struggling for an open harbor, and at last, after a seven years' fight, winning its cause, is analogous to the situation of numerous other American cities, that this story needs to be told in full, and to be given to the people in permanent book form.

It is the established policy of this government to make such improvements in its rivers and lakes as may be needed for the interior commerce of the States, and to throw open the coast line, by the development of new harbors and the maintenance of those already in existence, for our own vessels and those of foreign nations. But there is in this policy no warrant for the attempt now and again made by designing corporations, to bribe communities into selling their

---

*The name by which this measure is generally known among the members of the House is "the Beef Barrel."

birthright of commercial freedom for the mess of pottage of a few hundred thousand dollars of government appropriation.

The consideration of such a topic comes not inopportunely at a time when corporate wealth is rapidly drawing together in giant combinations that are destined, beyond doubt, to play an important part in the legislation of the future. As these organizations increase in strength, and knit more closely the ties that hold them to one another, the American people as a whole are likely to undergo a series of trials similar to those that for the past three decades have beset the residents of California—particularly in the northern and central sections of the State—who know by hard experience what it means to be subject, in business matters to the control, and in politics to the influence, of one all-powerful corporation. The process by which the trusts are destined to be drawn into politics is as simple as it is inevitable. The people believe these combinations to be a source of harm, and they will demand the passage of laws, both by Congress and the state legislatures, that will accomplish their destruction. Will the trusts tamely submit? Not while the law of self-preservation continues in force; not while expert lobbyists may be had to hire; not while party workers of the mercenary class stand ready to control caucuses and primaries and secure the nomination of pliable men. The managers of trusts and corporations are, perhaps, quite as conscientious as other men. They may refuse to bribe officials; but there is nothing in our scheme of political morality to prevent them from assisting friends to political honors. If Congress and the state legislatures succeed in passing laws which are obnoxious to the trusts, then the latter will be "driven into politics" just as the Southern Pacific has been in California. Thus the experience of the people of this State may be, within a short time, repeated on a larger scale all over the Union.

Let it be understood at the outset, however, that this book is not conceived in any spirit of opposition to railways or corporations in general, nor with any animus against the Southern Pacific in particular. The writer will frankly admit that when the harbor contest was in progress, he was an active opponent of the railroad and its plans, and that he did what he could as a newspaper writer, and as an officer of the Chamber of Commerce, to assist the San Pedro location. But the struggle is now at an end. The "Free Harbor" is practically a *fait accompli;* for the contract has been let, the work is under way, and the government is completely and irrevocably committed to that site. The writer is, therefore, no longer in the situation which in former years befell the residents of Los Angeles, viz., to take one side or the other—for the lines of demarkation are now broken down and obliterated—but, on the contrary, he approaches this work in the spirit of the historian, who will do justice to both factions and will narrate the events just as they happened.

There is an impression among Eastern people that the residents of this State entertain a violent, unreasoning prejudice against the Southern Pacific railroad, and that populistic ideas are generally much in vogue among us. The latter belief has been strengthened and confirmed by the election of three Populists to Congress from Southern California districts. As a matter of fact, there are fewer populists in this section than in most of the western Congressional districts that cover agricultural territory, but by the hazard of fusion politics these nominations chanced to fall to the Populist party, which, in conjunction with the Democracy, won several elections. The people of this State, particularly those of the Southern section, are largely emigrants from other portions of the Union. Broadened by the experience that comes from travel and from living under different circumstances and institutions, they are less likely than people of a more conservative cast of life to yield to prejudice of any kind, least of all to a desire foolishly to oppose the railroad that first connected their adopted home with Eastern civilization. It is true that there existed at one time in the State, with its active headquarters in San Francisco, an element which was known as the "Sand Lot"—a name which was given from the location where Denis Kearney, the agitator, was wont to hold his meetings; and the railroad was to this element the *bete noire* to which all the misfortunes that befell California in a time of a general financial depression were attributed. The

THE SAN PEDRO DEEP-WATER HARBOR AS IT WILL LOOK WHEN COMPLETED.
(1) Point Fermin. (2) San Pedro. (3) Terminal Island. (4) Long Beach. (5) Los Angeles. (6) Wilmington. (7) Terminal Railway.

days of Sand Lot meetings have long since passed, and, as if to point a happy moral, the very location where they were formerly held is now covered by beautiful buildings. The element that still bears the name has shrunk to insignificant proportions; its spirit is to be found only in the wild utterances of some political demagogue, or the reckless and extravagant denunciation of the railroad by some newspaper that seeks by that device to attract attention from the injudicious.*

---

*In the debate on the Santa Monica or San Pedro appropriation in the Senate, May 12th, 1896, Senator Perkins said, in discussing this topic of anti-railway prejudice in California:

I cannot permit to pass unchallenged the remarks made by the Senator from Missouri [Mr. Vest] and by the Senator from Maine [Mr. Frye].

The Senator from Missouri said: "Unfortunately Mr. Huntington is a political factor in California. They test every man's competency and qualification for office there by the question, 'Is he for Huntington or against him?' You can't hold a town meeting but what the question is, 'Is this man a Huntington man or not a Huntington man?'"

Then the Senator from Maine said, referring to some remarks which had been made by my distinguished colleague (Mr. White): "This savors of the slogan of the Sand Lots of the Golden Gate, where the name of Huntington is used to conjure with to frighten babies, and used by demagogues to make weak-kneed politicians tremble."

Mr. President, I dislike exceedingly to refer on this floor to any gentleman who is not a member of this body. . . . But I say that charge is a libel on the fair name of the good people of California, and I should be false to those I represent if I permitted the charge of the Senators from Maine and Missouri to pass unchallenged. The people of California have no prejudices against Mr. Huntington and his associates. I know nothing against Mr. Huntington to his discredit, unless it be his own testimony before a Congressional committee, and certain letters which, it is alleged, he wrote to an associate upon the board of directors of the company with which he was connected. . . . But I repel the charge that the people of California seek office by declaiming against him or his associates, or by advocating that which he desires, or by opposing it. . .

Mr. President, the people of California in city, county and state, gave most liberally toward building the first Transcontinental railroad. They were in sympathy with the promoters, because the latter were in touch with the people at that time; and if today our people censure them, it is because they believe they have not been true to their trust; that they have forgotten the common interests and the common bond which unite their interests with the interests of the people of California. That is the reason. If they are censured it is because they use their great power sometimes to thwart the wishes and desires of the people; but that the name of Mr. Huntington is used to influence the acts of public men in California is untrue.

The responsible men of California, who are blessed with brains and conscience, are not "against the Southern Pacific", although they are at times compelled to oppose that corporation in what it seeks to do. As American citizens, they naturally resent the presence in California politics of this sinister force; they are, however, too fair-minded to deny that the railroad is often driven into the political arena

C. P. HUNTINGTON.

in self-defense against legislative freebooters. Such men will deplore the indiscriminate attacks that are made on the railroad, and at the same time will be firm in protecting the people's interests when the corporation seeks to overreach them. If this constitutes "prejudice", so be it; but it is a prejudice in favor of his own honest rights, which the Californian shares with all his brethren of the Anglo-Saxon race.

The present narration has to deal with a contest which was waged through a period of about eight years in the city of

Los Angeles and in the Nation's capital, on the question of the location of a harbor to accommodate the commercial interests of the Southwest. The Southern Pacific railroad desired the harbor to be situated at Port Los Angeles, which is near the town of Santa Monica. The engineering authorities of the National Government had selected San Pedro as the most available spot, and that location was favored by the people of Los Angeles, or by a majority of them at least, because its water front was free and accessible to any number of railroads, or private individuals, that might choose to build wharves out into the harbor. Whether or not the harbor at Port Los Angeles could be successfully invaded by railroads competing with the Southern Pacific, was a moot question, upon which most of the discussion of the issue turned. The reader shall presently be put in possession of the evidence and the argument on both sides. Certain it is, however that the people of Los Angeles and the surrounding country—those whose interest in the question was most direct and profound—believed that the Port Los Angeles plan called for a monopoly harbor, and the fight was made on that basis. After a long and determined struggle, in the midst of which the cause of the people seemed many times to have suffered hopeless defeat, a victory was finally won for the San Pedro location. An appropriation of nearly $3,000,000 was secured and the work was inaugurated.

This, in a nutshell, is the incident which this book will describe in such detail as may be necessary to give the reader a clear idea what a fight between the people on the one side and a determined corporation on the other is like. As we have observed before, fights of this description may become painfully common during the next half-century, and their polemics will be a legitimate field of study.

A contest of such magnitude, extending through a long period of years, and involving to some degree every element of the community, could not fail to impress a lasting mark upon the character of a youthful city. One may speak of Los Angeles as youthful, for, although it was founded by the Spaniards over a century ago, it is, in every other respect than that of history, but twenty years old. Of those who now make up its population probably 85 per cent are newcomers since 1887. Los Angeles may therefore be regarded as in the early stages of a lusty youth, when character is most subject to influence by outward circumstance. To one who has traveled among American cities, or is acquainted with their intimate history, the mere mention of their names suggests their several peculiarities, as clearly defined as those of well known men or women. Thus, Boston expresses culture, Philadelphia conservatism and regard for family, New York elegance and a certain aristocratic complacency, and Chicago is synonymous with enterprise. Los Angeles is destined to be one of the great cities of the Union. Its growth from 11,000 in 1880 to 120,000 at the present time is a clear indication of its future. It will doubtless have, and to some extent it has already, those definite characteristics that will give it individuality among its sister cities. It is safe to say that the part Los Angeles has played, in this long and bitter struggle with a corporation which up to this time has been practically invincible, a struggle wherein the most powerful influences were brought to bear, and the strongest sentiments of the people were aroused, must have helped to develop in the city those traits of courage and perseverance that are the groundwork of all human success. If this be true, then the San Pedro contest has brought a double victory.

CHAPTER II.

Why the Harbor Was Needed.

THE industrial history of the United States up to the end of this century may be divided into two epochs: First, the agricultural period, when the chief effort of the people was to develop the resources of the soil, and second, the manufacturing period. To them is about to succeed a commercial period, when the genius of the American people will be devoted to the problem of marketing our surplus products in foreign countries and to the securing of our share in the carrying trade of the world. By the middle of this century the United States was the greatest producer of agricultural commodities on the globe. At the end of the century, it leads all other countries in manufacturing; and early in the twentieth century it will—unless all signs fail—attain its legitimate supremacy in commerce.

Twenty-five years ago we were exporting each year half a billion dollars worth of our products and importing goods to about the same value. Now we are exporting over a billion dollars worth annually, while the imports have increased but little. What relation manufacturing bears to this prosperous showing is revealed by the presence of such items as these in the list for 1898: Agricultural implements $7,609,000, Copper manufactures $32,180,000, Bicycles $6,846,000, Iron and steel products $70,406,000, Leather and leather articles $21,113,000, Hog products $110,801,000, Flour $69,263,000, Wooden manufactures $37,513,000.

On the other hand, when we consider the part played by this country in the world's carrying trade, we note that in 1860 the tonnage of American vessels amounted to 5,299,175 against 5,710,968 of Great Britain and 4,000,000 of all other countries. In 1890 the figures were, United States 4,424,497, Great Britain 11,597,106 and other countries 7,000,000; and at present United States 4,769,020, Great Britain 13,641,116, Germany 2,006,950 and all other countries 7,000,000. When it is remembered that 90 per cent of the American tonnage is engaged in domestic or coastwise trade, it will be seen that our vessels cut an almost insignificant figure in the world's commerce.

These facts, which are not particularly gratifying to the American's patriotism, are quoted merely to show how we have, in our devotion to the manufacturing interests of the country, overlooked the commercial. While other nations have fostered and encouraged by legislation and by force of a patriotic sentiment the building of ships and the development of deep-sea trade, we have turned all our energies toward that which we seemed chiefly to need, to-wit, manufacturing; and the splendidly profitable work of carrying the world's commodities from one nation to another, and, indeed, between our own nation and others has been allowed to drift entirely away from us.

But it is not alone the carrying trade that we have neglected, until it is lost and may be won back only by a hard struggle; we have lost, with respect to many countries, the very trade itself. To fail to hold our place in the rank of transporters is one thing; to suffer good markets to remain closed to us through indifference and mismanagement is another and a more serious one. The man who fails to earn the money that is legitimately his is the loser thereby, quite as much as he who parts with the same amount on some unlucky venture.

This has particular application to our trans-Pacific commerce. The oriental countries of China, Japan, British Australasia, Corea and Siberian Russia, the Philippines and the French and Dutch East Indies, lie nearer to the United States by a thousand miles or more than they do to Europe. These countries contain over 800,000,000 of population, and their area exceeds that of Europe and the United States combined. Their capacity for commerce, both as to what they produce for exportation and what they need to buy in return, is almost unlimited, although it has been as yet but partially developed. The real awakening of Japan has occurred only within the last ten years. That country, with a population of 41,000,000 and an area of 147,000 square miles, receives and sends out $280,000,000 worth of products each year, and of this the United States handles little less than one-fourth. When the same awakening comes to China with its 4,000,000 square miles and 400,000,000 of population, and to Siberian Russia, whose 6,500,000 square miles of territory are now being penetrated with a vast railway system that will bring its products out to Pacific waters at Vladivostock, what splendid opportunities will then be presented for American thrift and energy to create for this nation a commercial empire in the Orient!

The present commerce of the trans-Pacific countries is estimated at $2,000,000,000 annually. We import from those countries $150,000,000 each year and export to them $65,000,000. The disparity in these figures is all the more glaring when we compare them with the totals of our own exports and imports, which show that while twenty-five per cent of our total imports come from the Orient, but five per cent of our exports go to those shores. In short, the money that we pay the Mongolian for his curios and mattings, his teas and silks, goes to Europe to buy him woolens and canned goods and machinery. The United States, which is the legitimate and natural commercial ally of the whole Orient, is today receiving but seven per cent of its business, the remaining ninety-three per cent going largely to England, France and Germany, on the far opposite side of the globe.

Two events that took place in the year 1898 presaged the end of this anomalous condition of affairs. These were the battle of Manila Bay, May 1st, and the formal annexation of the Hawaiian Islands, August 12th. The United States is no longer a stranger in the Orient; it is now a free-holder there, and will maintain its right to all privileges, commercial and otherwise, that such rank conveys. Up to last year our exports to the Philippines averaged a little over $100,000 annually, as against nearly $20,000,000 which they paid to Spain for its products. In an open market, practically all of that business would come to us. With Manila for a base of operations, American business skill and enterprise will push its way into every corner of the Orient, and when the inevitable awakening comes to those vast hordes, they will minister to our needs, and we to theirs. The two billions of commerce will expand to three or four, and the gain will be largely to America.

Having considered the opportunity, let us now inquire into the facilities which we possess for meeting it. Unlike the Atlantic, the Pacific ocean is provided by nature with but few ports that are adapted to deep-sea commerce. The Puget Sound country has two, in Seattle and Tacoma; and the Columbia River presents a third at Portland. The Bay of San Francisco constitutes an excellent natural harbor; but south of that city for six hundred miles, the coast is inhospitable to the ocean-going vessel, until San Diego is reached, at the extreme southwestern corner of the Union.

The Northern Pacific and the Great Northern railways, and the Union Pacific, through the Oregon Short Line and Oregon Railway and Navigation Company's lines, carry the Oriental products that come into the three Northern ports, across the Western States to the Twin Cities and to Chicago, and the East. The Southern and Central Pacific (two routes of the same system) perform that service for San Francisco; and the Santa Fe for San Diego. The recent purchase by the Santa Fe of the Valley Railroad, which was an independent line built chiefly by the subscriptions of San Francisco people, through the San Joaquin Valley along the middle of the State, puts that great system, which has exercised such an important influence in the upbuilding of the southern section of California, into the city of the Golden Gate. Within a few months—certainly before the end of 1899—San Francisco will enjoy the advantage for which she has so long clamored, of competition in railroad transportation. It is safe to predict, however, that under the highly amicable arrangement that at present prevails between the Southern Pacific and the Santa Fe, no sudden change will occur in the commercial fortunes of that city.

The Oriental business is at the present time done almost entirely through the three northwestern ports and San Francisco. The harbor of San Diego, while it is of sufficient depth for trans-Pacific trade, has thus far remained practically undeveloped, although a regular line of steamers from that port to Yokohama has recently started into operation. Overtures have at various times been made to the San Diego people by the proprietors of Japanese lines, but satisfactory arrangements could not be effected. The difficulties in the way were, first, that the country immediately surrounding San Diego does not produce, in any quantity, the commodities which are needed for the return cargo, and, second, its railway facilities, as determined by location, grades, etc., do not admit of its competition with the other deep-sea harbors of the coast. These are difficulties which will be overcome in time, as the country about San Diego develops, and other railway lines are secured. That it is destined to be one of the great shipping points of the Pacific coast, no one can doubt.

There are now 2,000 arrivals of ships annually at the ports in Puget Sound, and 1,300 annually at Portland, in the Columbia river. San Francisco bay, which has served as the western terminus of a transcontinental line since 1865, and which is most favorably located of all the ports, greets 2,200 ships annually. These figures do not, of course, include coast trade, which does not bear on the present discussion. The freight that comes in is tea, rice, sugar (from Hawaii), silks, curios, tropical fruits; that which goes out is flour, canned goods, hog products and cotton.

Now, as the Pacific coast country, measuring it clear back to the Rockies, contains only two millions of people, scattered over seven hundred thousand square miles, it is clear enough that but a small fraction of this commerce is local. The curios are sold in Chicago and the East; the silks go on to New York and are scattered all over the country; and, on the other hand, the hog products come from Kansas City and Omaha; the flour, much of it, comes from Minnesota, and the cotton from Texas. The Pacific coast is, therefore, merely the gateway by which the commercial interests of the Middle and Eastern States pass over to the Orient.

Commerce, like most other natural forces, will follow the line of least resistance, and there enter, as material factors in the railway end of the calculation, questions of distance, grade, snow, and, sometimes, most important of all, opportunity for competition. When the cotton of Texas, grown in latitude 30 deg., is carried north to latitude 47 deg.—a matter of 2000 miles as the railroad runs—subsequently to be delivered at Hong-Kong, latitude 23 deg., it is a paradox that must some day be abolished. By all the laws of logic and good business sense, cotton should seek its outlet to the Pacific at the nearest practicable point. Moreover, the heavy and costly freight which comes to this country from the Orient should not be sent across the continent over steep grades and through snow blockades, if level and clear routes are to be had.

The city of Los Angeles, which, being within a few miles of the coast, we may regard as a Pacific terminus, marks the western end of the shortest route over the most practical gradients between the Atlantic and Pacific waters. It is north from San Diego over 100 miles, south from San Francisco 500 miles. In all that distance of over 600 miles, there is no harbor where deep-sea vessels may enter, either to seek refuge from a storm or deliver a cargo. A corresponding distance on the Atlantic coast would be from Portland, Maine, to Cape May, or from Dover to Charleston. Three railway routes lead out from Los Angeles across the continent: The Southern Pacific and Central and Union Pacific roads together constitute one line; the Southern Pacific, and Texas and Missouri Pacific another; and the Santa Fe system, a direct through line practically under one ownership into Chicago, is the third. The latter road was built in competition with the other two, and for a number of years

THE OUTLETS TO TRANS-PACIFIC COMMERCE.

rivalry was active, contributing in a marked degree to the progress of the adjacent country.*

Thus the enterprise of the railway builder was united with the favoring influence of nature, to mark this as the proper location for a harbor for the southwestern coast of the Union—not in opposition to any other ports now existing on the Pacific coast, but in addition to and supplementing them. There will be work enough developed for all within the next ten years, and each will serve its own territory.

Although the Pacific ocean is not as restless as the Atlantic, there was ample justification for the building of a harbor at some point near Los Angeles for the refuge of storm-beleagured vessels. On this topic Senator Frye of Maine, who has for many years served as Chairman of the Senate Committee on Commerce, said: "It [the proposed harbor in the vicinity of Los Angeles] is for the commerce of the world, and not only is it for the commerce of the world, but it is for a harbor of refuge, just as important as a harbor for commerce. The Atlantic coast has harbors of refuge all along. We are building one now at Sandy Bay, on the New England coast at a cost of $5,000,000, and we have them every forty or fifty miles: harbors to which tempest-tossed ships can run for refuge. They are just as important for protection to life and property as are protected harbors for commerce."

It would seem that if the Government could afford to build harbors of refuge every fifty miles along the Atlantic coast, some of them at a cost as great as $5,000,000, there was ample warrant for the expenditure of the $2,900,000 which was finally appropriated for San Pedro, to construct one harbor in a stretch of over 600 miles; and of this sum less than half, it appears, is called for by the actual contracted work.

However, it was not for a harbor of refuge nor for one of naval necessity that Los Angeles ten years ago first presented its claims for the construction of a great sea-wall at San Pedro. It was in order that the work begun by nature might

---

* To these routes may be added a third, projected to run from Salt Lake City to Los Angeles, shorter and more direct than any of the others and over easy grades through a productive country. It is now but a question of a short time when this road will be constructed.

be completed in the making of a port for the commerce of the Orient, a large portion of which should by the operation of the inevitable laws of trade gravitate to this region. It was that the cotton of the South and the hams and bacon of Kansas and the fabrics and machinery of the East might find their way, by easy grades and cheap transportation, to the Pacific, where they would join with the wheat and flour and fruit and canned goods of California, and embark for shipment across to the countries of the Orient; and that in return should come the silks and tea and rice and the handiwork of the East to be distributed over the same route back into the center of the nation. Many times in the struggle was the question to be met: "What need has Los Angeles for this harbor?" to which the answer was always given: "It is the United States that needs it."

CHAPTER III.

THE ANCIENT PORT OF SAN PEDRO.

IT was in 1542, thirty-six years after the death of the discoverer of the Americas, that Cabrillo, a Spanish navigator, sailing under the flag of the great Emperor, Charles V, entered the bay of San Pedro; and the Indians who inhabited the islands and the adjoining mainland, in great numbers and in appalling wretchedness, gazed, for the first time, on Caucasian faces. It was, perhaps, in honor of the arrival of these godlike beings, with their bird-winged conveyance, that the savages set fire to the dry grass of the plains along the shore; and the great clouds of smoke which overhung the land caused Cabrillo to give the place the name of Bahia de los Humos—the Bay of Smokes.

Historically, therefore, San Pedro is entitled to take precedence over any port on the Atlantic coast. At the time of its discovery, Henry VIII of England was busy intriguing for a new wife, Germany was in the midst of the fierce religious wars that grew out of the Reformation, the massacre of St. Bartholomew had not yet taken place in France, De Soto was just making his way up into the Mississippi, and the father of William Shakespeare was courting Mary Arden. It was not until sixty-seven years later that Henry Hudson ascended the river that bears his name, in the search for a northwest passage, and gave the title of New Amsterdam to the future site of the great metropolis; and when the first English settlement was effected on American soil, San Pedro had been on the navigator's map over half a century. The name San Pedro was bestowed in honor of St. Peter, Bishop of Alexandria, on whose day, November 28th, Viscaino, who succeeded Cabrillo in the exploration of this coast, first entered the harbor, in 1603. That is the name which is applied to the exterior roadstead or bay; the interior bay or lagoon is officially known as Wilmington. There is a town of San Pedro, which is situated on and about the bluffs behind Point Fermin,* and there is also a town of Wilmington, which is two miles farther to the north and east, at the head of the lagoon. Both of these towns, however, are matters of the last half century.

Up to the time of the founding of the chain of missions in California by the Franciscan fathers, which occurred in the period from 1769 to 1800, the harbor or roadstead of San Pedro was entered only at rare intervals by craft of any description. When the mission of San Gabriel was established thirty miles to the north, and the pueblo of Los Angeles was founded, which events took place about 1780, the first real commerce of San Pedro began. Before twenty years had passed, the mission was enjoying a high degree of prosperity, and the pueblo had grown to be the largest settlement on the Pacific coast. Tens of thousands of cattle roamed through the San Gabriel and San Fernando Valleys, herded by Indians under the guardianship of the Mission padres, and the hides and tallow of these cattle formed the staple export of the country, in return for which the Yankee trading vessels that frequented the coast brought cloth and sugar and household goods of every kind.

---

*There are three recognized spellings for Point Fermin. The Board of 1890 calls it "Firmen." The local mapmakers generally put it "Fermin." The Walker Board spells it "Firmin" in the text of the report or "Fermin" on the maps. The army authorities generally call it "Fermin", and so does the Coast Survey. Mariner's Charts generally print it "Firmen." About the only way successfully to misspell it is "Fermen," an achievement that is witnessed occasionally in the newspapers.

In 1835, when the Mission regime was at its best, Richard H. Dana visited this coast, in the capacity of a common sailor, on board the brig Pilgrim. He spent two years cruising up and down among the harbors of California, and his impressions are graphically set forth in his "Two Years Before the Mast", which is a true book of the sea, and a literary masterpiece as well. He gives an entertaining description of the roadstead of San Pedro and of the way in which commerce was carried on through California ports at that time, over sixty years ago:

"Leaving Santa Barbara, we coasted along down, the country appearing level or moderately uneven, and for the most part, sandy and treeless; until, doubling a high sandy point, we let go anchor at a distance of three and a half miles from shore. It was like a vessel bound for St. John's, Newfoundland, coming to anchor on the Grand Banks; for the shore, being low, appeared to be at a greater distance than it actually was, and we thought we might as well have stayed at Santa Barbara, and sent down our boat for the hides.

"The land was of a clayey quality, and as far as the eye could reach, entirely bare of trees and even shrubs; there was no sign of a town—not even a house to be seen. What brought us into such a place, we could not conceive.

"No sooner had we come to anchor, than the slip-rope, and the other preparations for southeasters, were got ready; and there was reason enough for it, for we lay exposed to every wind that could blow, except the northerly winds, and they came over a flat country with a rake of more than a league of water.

"The boat was lowered, and as we drew in, we found the tide low, and the rocks and stones covered with kelp and seaweed, lying bare for the distance of nearly half a mile. Leaving the boat, and picking our way barefooted over these, we came to what is called the landing place, at high-water mark. The soil was, as it appeared at first, loose and clayey, and except the stalks of the mustard plant, there was no vegetation. Just in front of the landing, and immediately over it, was a small hill, which, from its being not more than forty or fifty feet high, we had not perceived from our anchorage.

"Over this hill we saw three men coming down, dressed partly like sailors and partly like Californians. When they reached us, we found that they were Englishmen. They told

us that they had belonged to a small Mexican brig which had been driven ashore here in a southeaster, and now lived in a small house over the hill. Going up this hill with them, we saw, close behind it, a small low building, with one room, containing a fireplace, cooking apparatus, etc., and the rest of it unfurnished, and used as a place to store hides and goods. This, they told us, was built by some traders in the Pueblo (a town about thirty miles in the interior, to which this was the port) and used by them as a store-house, and also as a lodging-place when they came down to trade with the vessels. The nearest house, they told us, was a Rancho, or cattle farm, about three miles off.

"I learned, to my surprise, that this desolate looking place furnished more hides than any port on the coast. It was the only port for a distance of eighty miles, and about thirty miles in the interior was a fine plain country, filled with herds of cattle, in the center of which was the Pueblo of Los Angeles—the largest town in California—and several of the largest missions; to all of which San Pedro was the seaport.

"The next day we pulled the agent ashore, and he went up to visit the Pueblo and the neighboring missions; and in a few days, as the result of his labors, large oxcarts, and droves of mules, loaded with hides, were seen coming over the flat country.

"We loaded our long-boat with goods of all kinds, light and heavy, and pulled ashore. After landing and rolling them over the stones on the beach, we stopped, waiting for the carts to come down the hill and take them; but the captain soon settled the matter by ordering us to carry them all up to the top, saying that was the 'California fashion.' So what the oxen would not do, we were obliged to do. The hill was low, but steep, and the earth being clayey and wet with recent rains, was bad holding ground for our feet. The heavy barrels and casks we rolled up with some difficulty, getting behind and putting our shoulders to them; now and then our feet slipping, added to the danger of the casks rolling back upon us. But the greatest trouble was the large boxes of sugar. These we had to place upon oars, and lifting them up, rest the oars upon our shoulders, and creep slowly up the hill with the gait of a funeral procession.

"After an hour or two of hard work, we got them all up, and found the carts standing full of hides, which we had to unload, and to load the carts again with our own goods; the lazy Indians, who came down with them, squatting on their hams, looking on, doing nothing, and when we asked them to help us, only shaking their heads, or drawling out 'no quiero.'

"Having loaded the carts, we started up the Indians, who went off, one on each side of the oxen, with long sticks sharpened at the end, to punch them with. This is one of the means of saving labor in California—two Indians to two oxen.

"Now, the hides were to be got down; and for this purpose we brought the boat around to a place where the hill was steeper, and threw them off, letting them slide over the slope. Many of them lodged, and we had to let ourselves down and set them going again, and in this way we became covered with dust, and our clothes torn. After we had the hides all down, we were obliged to take them on our heads, and walk over the stones, and through the water, to the boat. The water and the stones together would wear out a pair of shoes a day, and as shoes were very scarce and very dear, we were compelled to go barefooted.

"At night we went on board, having had the hardest and most disagreeable day's work that we had yet experienced. For several days we were employed in this manner, until we had landed forty or fifty tons of goods, and brought on board about two thousand hides, when the trade began to slacken. On Thursday night there was a violent blow from the northward; but as this was off shore, we had only to let go our other anchor and hold on."

In a postscript to "Two Years," written a quarter of a century later, in 1859, Dana describes a visit which he made to San Pedro at that time. "I could scarce recognize the hill up which we rolled and dragged and pushed our heavy loads," says he, "It was no longer the landing place. One had been made at the head of the creek, and boats discharged and took off cargoes from a mole or wharf, in a quiet place, safe from southeasters. A tug ran to take off passengers from the steamer to the wharf—for the trade of Los Angeles is sufficient to support such a vessel. I walked along the shore to the new landing place, where there were two or three store-houses and other buildings, fronting a small depot; and a stage coach, I found, went daily between this place and the Pueblo."

The "creek" to which Dana refers is the estuary, which is now generally described as the "inner harbor." This estuary had, at the time of which Dana writes in his postscript, a channel about two miles long and 100 feet wide and from 6 to 10 feet deep at mean low tide, sufficient for the accommodation of lighters, barges, tugs and small coast vessels. At the mouth of the estuary, and cutting it off from the outer bay, there was a bar where the water measured only 18 inches at low tide. The use of the inner area was, therefore limited to such boats as could get over the bar at high tide. The tides in this port vary between 4½ and 7 feet.

This estuary was formed by the mainland on the west side, and by the long low strip of sand-dunes formerly known as Rattlesnake Island, and now called Terminal Island, on the east. Between the latter and Deadman's Island lay about 3000 feet of flats, partly submerged even at low water. In the map which accompanies this narration, these flats do not appear; for it was along the line where they formerly lay that the jetty was built by the government: the work which was begun in the year 1871. Extensive flats also surrounded the estuary to the east and west in the vicinity of the town of Wilmington. The total area covered by the sea at high tide inside the bar was about 1500 acres.

The roadstead lying without the bar was protected on the west by the headland of Point Fermin and on the south and southwest, to some extent, by the island of Catalina, twenty miles away. To the east and north lay the mainland. There was no protection whatever from storms coming from the southeast; and it is in that quarter that the storms of winter originate on this portion of the Pacific coast. During the greater part of the year, however, the roadstead afforded good anchorage and fair protection to vessels, and even prior to the improvement of the estuary, a very considerable volume of coast commerce was carried on through the port of San Pedro. By 1869 this business had grown so considerable as to justify the building of a railway line between San Pedro and Los Angeles, which was the first piece of railroad constructed in Southern California. This line, 23 miles in length, was subsequently acquired by the Southern Pacific, when that corporation entered this territory in 1876, and is today a branch of the latter system.

In addition to the official report made by Williamson as above noted, an official examination and report was made by Gen. Barton S. Alexander a year later, and concurrent resolutions passed the Legislature asking for an appropriation based on Alexander's Report.

CHAPTER IV.

Work on the Interior Harbor.

ESTUARIES, similar to that of San Pedro or Wilmington, are to be found all over the world; and their improvement into harbors of greater or less efficiency conforms to a well established and thoroughly understood law. The rising and falling of the tide, which occurs twice in every twenty-four hours, carries a great volume of water in and out of the mouth of the estuary, and this, if properly confined, and directed, may be used to scour out a channel for the entrance of ships.

The conditions presented by the estuary which we are considering, were unusually favorable. The tidal area, that is to say, the extent of the land covered by water at mean high tide, was very large in proportion to the width of the channel at the mouth, provided the channel was confined to its proper limits and the leaks—so to speak—stopped up. The tide water, which amounted on the average to about 250,000,000 cubic feet, passed in and out over the flats that lay between Deadman's Island and Rattlesnake Island on the one side, and along the mainland at Point Fermin on the other side. The current was slow and without force, and the sand at the bottom of the channel and on the bar was disturbed but little. But if confined and made to work in a narrow channel, this great volume of water would exert a dredging power of splendid proportions, and the sand once thrown out beyond the bar into the ocean, it would be picked up by the side currents and carried away from the mouth of the harbor. The problem presented at San Pedro was not complicated—as the case has frequently been elsewhere—by the presence of a river of fresh water flowing into the estuary and carrying down a great quantity of silt and sediment to clog up the harbor. Doubtless in some earlier geological period, when rains fell in great volume in California, instead of sparsely as at present, the Wilmington lagoon was the outlet for a great river, probably the San Gabriel, and in that way the estuary first formed. At present the San Gabriel

THE HARBOR FROM DEAD MANS ISLAND, SHOWING JETTY WORK.

VIEW OF INTERIOR HARBOR.

THE FIRST APPROPRIATION.

has its principal outlet about ten miles to the southward of San Pedro; but at the time the harbor was constructed the river discharged the main portion of its waters into the Wilmington estuary, though it was only after seasons of unusual rainfall, and then only for a period of a few weeks, that this discharge materially affected the regular volume of the tidal prism that daily found its way down to the sea.

The first appropriation for the improvement of the inner harbor passed March 2, 1871. The amount was $200,000

COL. S. O. HOUGHTON.

on a project that called for a total expenditure of $530,000, and that contemplated a depth of ten feet of water at mean low tide.

Los Angeles at that time was a city of about 8,000 population, not more than twenty per cent of whom were Americans. It had no railway connection with the East; and it was not until five years later that the Southern Pacific came over the Tehachapi Pass into the Southern valleys. The surrounding country was but little improved, the land being used chiefly for grazing. The status of Southern California is very plainly shown in the name, which was then generally applied to it, of the "cow counties." All the southern and central sections of the State were included in one congressional district, whose representative at that time was Col. S. O. Houghton, of San Jose. Col. Houghton is now a resident of Los Angeles and a prominent member of the bar of that city. Through him the first appropriation for San Pedro was secured.*

Agitation in favor of the improvement of the Wilmington lagoon, to accomplish such a deepening of the main channel as would admit coasting vessels of light draft, had been under way for some time. The prospect of securing connection by railway with the Eastern states was then considered very distant. Only one transcontinental line, the Union and Central Pacific, existed, as against the seven that now cross the country. That one had been constructed under such tremendous difficulties, and was operated at such expense, as to render a second project, especially one over the lower and desolate southern route, extremely dubious. The necessity for a water connection between Los Angeles and the outer world was therefore most urgent; the development of the section seemed to depend absolutely upon it.

The number of far-sighted enterprising men in Los Angeles at that time must have been very small, however, for the project to improve San Pedro excited but languid interest, and was openly opposed in some quarters. Col. G. H. Mendell, who was in charge of the work from the beginning, is authority for the statement that many of the old settlers regarded the undertaking with contempt, and "figured" that the government must have a great deal of money to waste, if it could spend so many thousands of dollars on a useless mud hole like the Wilmington lagoon.

The first authoritative report on the possibilities of the inner harbor was made in 1869, by Major R. S. Williamson, of the U. S. Corps of Engineers, who, in response to an

---

* Col. Houghton was one of the earliest advocates, if not the earliest, of deep-water development in the outside harbor, and in the last year of his term procured the passage of a recommendation to the U. S. Engineering Department that a survey be made of the roadstead as to its possibilities.

urgent petition from Pheneas Banning, Don Benito Wilson and others, made a careful examination and survey of the estuary and submitted plans and a project for its improvement the following year. Representative Houghton, who had visited San Pedro the previous year, and had at that time proposed to the active citizens of Los Angeles the possibility of securing government aid for the undertaking,

COL. GEORGE H. MENDELL.
Corps of Engineers U. S. A. (Retired.)

went before the River and Harbor committee in the session of 1870-1, and obtained an appropriation of $200,000 to begin the work.

The first project which called, as has been said, for a total expenditure of $430,000, contemplated the removal of the shoal at the entrance of the channel and the straightening and deepening of the latter. This was to be accomplished by the extension of Rattlesnake Island to Deadman's Island by filling the intervening distance, 6700 feet, with rock and timbers, in which, it was expected, the sand would lodge, making a solid, impenetrable wall. By this process the great volume of tide water that had heretofore escaped over the flats would be restrained in the channel, and, flowing out in a swift current, would scour away the bottom to the desired depth. Some dredging and blasting of the channel was also contemplated as part of the work.

Some difficulties were encountered, but the results realized were all and even more than had been predicted. June 1, 1872, Congress made a second appropriation, this time of $75,000 and again about a year later of $150,000, thus making a total of $425,000, which was about all that had been asked. Col. Mendell then proceeded to devise a new project for the further continuance of the work. This called for the building up of the east jetty to a higher level and its extension beyond Deadman's Island for about 400 feet, and for the building up and further construction of the jetty on the west side of the channel to a length of about 3500 feet, which would cut off the flats on that side, and quicken the tidal current as it passed over the bar.

The appropriations under this second project came slowly and the work dragged, with a great sacrifice of economy and a postponement of the desired results. The amounts and dates were as follows: 1875, $30,000, 1878, $20,000, 1879, $12,000, 1880, $35,000, 1881, $33,000, 1882, $100,000, 1884, $50,000, 1886, $75,000, 1888, $90,000, 1890, $34,000, 1892, $50,000. Had the latter portion of the work been pushed with the same activity as the former, the government would have been the gainer in many thousands of dollars, and the people of this section would have enjoyed the use of the inner harbor at a much earlier date.

The results finally attained through these expenditures exceeded the best that had been expected. The various boards of expert engineering authorities, which have considered the case of San Pedro on numerous occasions since this work came to an end, have all, without exception, commented with surprise on the admirable results attained through Col. Mendell's project.

An excellent description of the inner harbor work, and the changed conditions at the port on its completion, is to be found in an address delivered in 1891 before the Chamber of Commerce of Los Angeles, by Captain James J. Meyler, the supervising engineer. From that the following is quoted:

"The channel has deepened, widened and straightened. Where we had depths from 6 to 10 feet in 1871, we have now from 16 to 22 feet, and the depth of 18 inches on the bar has increased to at least 14 feet. There are at present lying along side the wharves in the inner harbor two four-masted schooners and a barkentine, which had draughts, when crossing the inner bar, of 17 feet 8 inches, 18 feet 6 inches, and 18 feet 3 inches, respectively. Up to the present time about 133,000 tons of stone have been placed in the breakwaters, and there have been excavated only about 177,000 cubic yards of material, about 58,000 cubic yards of which was stone from a ledge of rock crossing the channel at the

CAPT. JAMES J. MEYLER,
Corps of Engineers U. S. A.

inner bar. From a rough calculation, however, I estimate that at least 2,000,000 cubic yards of material have been removed from the channel, over nine-tenths of which has been done independently of dredging or blasting, the result of construction alone—the channel scouring itself under the action of natural causes. The improvements have rendered it possible for the usual trading vessels of the coast to enter at this point a safe inclosed anchorage, free of all exposure to storms, and to deliver freight without the use of lighters.

The total number of tons of exports and imports has increased tenfold since 1871; the collections of the port of Wilmington since 1882 have almost paid for the government construction and work in the harbor, and the present rates of 50 cents per 1,000 feet of lumber and 75 cents per ton of merchandise were $7.50 and $5.00 respectively in 1871."

In the years 1886, 1887, 1888 there occurred in Southern California a sudden growth in population, which led to a number of interesting industrial changes, the whole phenomenon receiving, by general consent, the name of "The Boom." So important was the part played in the history of Los Angeles by this event, that the people have adopted it as a sort of a chronological datum plane; and everything is dated before or after "the Boom," just as in Chicago it is before and after "the Fire," or, in the South, "the War." When a sleepy village of 15,000 people is transformed in the brief space of about 20 months into a progressive city of over 50,000, and a sparsely settled district that contains but 70,000 people suddenly acquires over 200,000 population, extraordinary changes in real estate values, in commerce, and in the industries and habits of the people naturally ensue.

There is an impression in some quarters, particularly among persons who have paid a hasty visit to the coast, that this sudden inflation of values and rapid multiplying of interests in Southern California worked a lasting injury to the section. That is an error. On the contrary the real birth of the country into commercial and social importance dates from the epoch of "the boom." There were before that time, as we have already noted, progressive and active men in Southern California, and they made their influence felt to some extent; but they were too few in number to dominate the tone and sentiment of the community. The industries of the section were limited and feeble, the improvements insignificant, and the outlook not promising. But with the completion of a second transcontinental competing line into Los Angeles and San Diego, a vast tide of new immigration swept into Southern California from the thrifty middle Western States, and the whole aspect of the country changed.

It was in that period of sudden expansion when the people

began to understand the splendid possibilities of a region where an almost perfect climate combines with a fertile soil, within the limits of a free and enlightened nation—a combination to be found nowhere else in the world—that the idea of a deep-sea harbor of the first rank and magnitude came to be a practical issue in Los Angeles. Before that time it had been suggested, but only as a vague and distant futurity, like the building of the Nicaragua Canal or the redemption of the Mojave Desert. Col. Mendell says that he remembers discussing the subject in 1881 with Senator Stanford, who was the president of the Central and Southern Pacific railroads. The interview as related by Col. Mendell, in an article in the Los Angeles Times, contains much that is significant in its bearing on the present commercial situation, and it is entertaining, moreover, on account of the change in the attitude of the Southern Pacific after Mr. Huntington succeeded Senator Stanford in its management. The article reads as follows:

> The Southern Pacific railroad had then been recently finished, and its president expected that by reason of its light grades it must become the route of an immense commerce to be developed on the Asiatic shore. He [Gov. Stanford] expressed his intention to build steamers of capacity to carry 15,000 to 20,000 tons each. He stated that the commerce with China was in its infancy, and, considering its enormous population, he expected exchanges to take dimensions not then anticipated by any one. There were obvious and serious objections to San Francisco as the port for commerce to be handled over the Southern Pacific railroad, in that freight would have to be transported over nearly five hundred miles of railroad and pass three summits in order to reach Los Angeles. It was plain that these ships must receive and discharge their cargoes upon the adjacent coast, and his first inquiry was whether or not Wilmington harbor could be made to accommodate vessels of the proposed magnitude. The reply was that it was quite impracticable to make the estuary suitable for so large vessels. His next inquiry was as to an alternative harbor. San Diego had no railroad connection and could not be considered. He was informed that it would be quite practicable to build a breakwater in the bay of San Pedro, under the lee of which vessels of any size might lie in security in touch with the railroad and there receive and discharge cargoes. At a later

date he was given a map, which, in a general way, illustrated the project of an outer harbor.

That the idea of asking the government to undertake the construction of a deep-sea harbor for trans-Pacific commerce was not general until the lessons of "the boom" were learned, appears from a memorial to Congress isued by the Los Angeles Board of Trade in February of 1888, in which a modest request is put forth in behalf of an appropriation of $200,000 to complete the work on the interior harbor, with no mention of the deep-sea improvement. In this document there is reproduced, however, a letter from W. H. H. Benyaurd, Major (now Lieut.-Colonel) of Engineers U. S. Army, under date of Nov. 29, 1887, in which he states that a survey has just been completed "looking to the formation of an outer harbor at San Pedro Bay, for the protection of deep-draft vessels."

Although the work on the interior harbor was not completed at the time of "the boom", the effect on the shipping at that port may be seen from the figures of the duties collected before and during these eventful years:

YEAR	DUTIES	TONNAGE
1883	$ 38,911.87	$7988.70
1884	52,029.95	3290.48
1885	39,428.69	2100.27
1886	63,960.46	3922.47
1887	105,627.62	4598.49
1888	159,111.23	6235.56

In 1887, 889 vessels entered the port, of which 69 were from foreign countries, the remainder coasting craft. In 1888 the number ran to 1092, of which 105 were foreign. These were the palmy days of San Pedro, the time when its people thought, "full surely its greatness was a-ripening." In a year or two more, the two roadsteads to the north, Redondo and Santa Monica, were to be developed, and the coast business to be wrested away, and—bitterest of all—the railroad, which thus far had proved San Pedro's most powerful ally, was destined to transfer its allegiance to another quarter, and the ancient embarcadero was to pass for nearly a decade through a period of extreme tribulation. But the thought had been uttered that there should some day be a deep-sea harbor near Los Angeles for the trans-Pacific commerce of that city, the southwest, and all the Union. The seed was planted that was destined to grow and to bear splendid fruit.

CHAPTER V.
Enter the Chamber of Commerce.

IN the fall of 1888 an organization was formed in the city of Los Angeles which was to play an important part in the harbor contest—indeed it must be admitted that without this organization the victory could never have been won.

Most western cities have societies for local improvement which usually bear the name Board of Trade or Chamber of Commerce. Los Angeles had possessed various organizations of this character, which had sprung up from time to time, flourished for a short period, and then passed away. In the later 80's the Board of Trade, which had given some attention to public questions, decided to devote its strength to the special business interests of its members, and this left the city with no agency to look out for the general good.

On the suggestion of W. E. Hughes, Major E. W. Jones and S. B. Lewis a public meeting was held on October 11, 1888, when a plan was formulated for a Chamber of Commerce, an organization with a membership that should include not business men alone, but property owners and professional men as well—in short every one who was interested in the prosperity of Los Angeles and Southern California.

About 150 members were enrolled, each of whom paid an initiation fee of $5.00, and thereafter dues of $1.00 a month. On this small financial basis an institution began which has brought many millions of dollars into the country, and which has itself spent hundreds of thousands of dollars in advertising the section and assisting in its development. When the Chamber had been in existence four years it had a membership of over 500, from which it derived an income sufficient to maintain it in satisfactory style, while the money that was needed for active work was secured by subscription.

EXHIBIT ROOM OF THE LOS ANGELES CHAMBER OF COMMERCE.

In its third year the Chamber established the free exhibit of Southern California products, which comes very near to being the finest and largest display of that character to be found anywhere in the world. The only two that experienced travelers mention to compare with it are the Bourse Exhibit of Philadelphia and the Colonial Products display in London.

The present membership of the Chamber is over 1,000, and includes practically all the active business men, public-spirited property owners, and successful professional men in the city. It has also a considerable membership of notable men all over Southern California, and the various counties of the section participate in the display of products. The latter, which occupies the second and third stories of a building 120 feet square, is visited by nearly 100,000 people annually, hailing from every country on the globe.

In the eleven years that have elapsed since it came into existence, the Chamber has had entire charge of nearly all the notable public enterprises inaugurated in Los Angeles. It has sent exhibits in great quantities to fairs, and special displays all over the world, and its printed matter has gone forth by the carload. Los Angeles is certainly one of the best advertised cities in the Union, and it owes the splendid results that have followed, in the form of a desirable immigration and the influx of new capital, to the wisdom and energy of its leading commercial organization. At the time of the active harbor agitation, the Merchants and Manufacturers' Association, which has since achieved distinction for good public work, did not exist; the Chamber of Commerce stood alone, and represented as nothing else could, the active, progressive sentiment of the country. Great care had been used by the intelligent and conscientious men who made up its directorate—men who were for the most part re-elected year after year—to preserve the institution from any scandal of self-seeking or of personal ambition. As a consequence, it exercised an ascendency over public opinion, which, in a crisis, such as the city was about to meet, would prove of inestimable value.

It is necessary to speak thus in detail of the Chamber of Commerce, in order that the reader who is perhaps not a resident of Southern California, or who is a newcomer to this section, may appreciate its power and influence—so much beyond that which the mere name might suggest.

The first object of this organization, as set forth in its by-laws, is to foster the commerce of Los Angeles and Southern California; and, as a deep-water harbor was a primary necessity to the attainment of any foreign trade, to work for San Pedro—and up to 1892 no other location than San Pedro was seriously considered—became a fundamental article in the Chamber of Commerce creed. It was generally admitted, even by the most ardent harbor enthusiasts, that there was little hope of early results from that work. In the first place, the interior harbor was still unfinished, and the government was not likely to consider a new project, until it had completed the one in hand. Appropriations were coming slowly, and in such small amounts that the improvements barely held their own against the influences of nature. The amount which it was estimated would be required for the construction of the outer harbor was very large, and it must of necessity be considered by Congress all at once, under the continuing contract plan, as the work could not be done successfully in piece-meal appropriations. The totals of the river and harbor bills were increasing by giant strides each year, and a general outcry against such extravagance was heard all over the Union.

There had been up to this time no definite project devised by the engineering authorities of the government, but a semi-official suggestion had been offered that the construction of a sea wall, a breakwater of stone, running out from a point a little to the north of Point Fermin, about two miles in length, would probably accomplish what was desired. It was roughly estimated that this would cost between four and five millions of dollars. The vagueness of the whole calculation shows in the fact that when the work was actually let by contract, ten years later, the price agreed upon was $1,300,000. The cost of such work, however, has considerably diminished during that period.

In spite of this discouraging outlook the Chamber of Commerce went bravely to work to obtain, first of all, the appropriations that were needed to complete the inner harbor, and second, to secure a small appropriation for the preparing of a project on the deep-water plan.

A favorite method employed by the Chamber to push the harbor's interests was to seize upon any senator, or member of the House, or upon any person of influence who might be visiting the coast and convey him to San Pedro on a special train, accompanied by a number of enthusiastic harbor advocates, who made clear to him by ocular demonstration, backed up by statistics and an abundance of argument, the entire feasibility of the deep-water idea. It happened that during '88-'89 and '90 a number of congressional committees visited the coast. Senator Leland Stanford, who at that time was president of the Southern Pacific, always accompanied these parties, and was a hearty advocate of the claims of San Pedro. The section's representative in Congress, Gen. Vandever of Ventura, also assisted in the entertainment of these guests.

A notable incident took place, just at that time, which had no little bearing on the subsequent contest, in the visit paid by Senator Frye of Maine to Los Angeles and San Pedro. The Committee on Commerce of the Senate was making a tour of the country, to inspect the various harbor projects on which it was called to vote, and in October of 1889 came to the Pacific coast. The Maine Senator was chairman of the committee, and although not all its members were present, those who accompanied him to San Pedro were Dawes of Massachusetts, Platt of Connecticut, Davis of Minnesota, Morgan of Alabama, and Turpie of Indiana. There was a special train, containing about thirty members of the Chamber and a few representative people from San Diego.

In the contest between the people and the Southern Pacific railway over the location of the harbor, Senator Frye of Maine was, from beginning to end, an unwavering and determined opponent of San Pedro. His position as chairman of the Committee on Commerce made it possible for him to destroy, year after year, all chance of appropriation for that harbor, and he openly and without hesitation made use of that opportunity. Whenever the matter came up in the committee, he invariably took an active part in the discussion, denouncing the San Pedro location, even in the face of the engineers' repeated decisions, using all the arts of persuasion and cajolery (and those arts, with the chairman of the committee that passes on appropriations for every State in the Union, are most powerful), and even falling back on the infallible "Senatorial courtesy" when every other method failed for gaining delay. Alone and almost unaided, for a number of years, he succeeded in defeating every effort to get the question actually considered by Congress; and when at last, chiefly through the efforts of Senator White of Los Angeles, the issue was forced out of the committee into the open Senate, it was Mr. Frye of Maine who led the fight in behalf of the railroad's choice for a location, conferring frequently in the lobby and committee rooms of the Senate with Mr. Huntington and his body-guard of workers. There were, it may be admitted, a number of supporters of the Santa Monica site who approached the question in a judicial spirit, and who believed with all sincerity that the Government engineers were in error, but Mr. Frye, as his every utterance on the harbor issue showed plainly enough, was a partisan of the most persistent and uncompromising type.

There has been much speculation among the people of Southern California, who were interested in the fate of the harbor, as to the reason for Mr. Frye's extraordinary attitude. Men who occupy positions of public trust sometimes favor rich corporations with their votes, because they sincerely believe in the justice of the cause; but the public servant that becomes their open and avowed advocate, and devotes his energies to their interests with the active zeal of a faithful attorney, must expect to encounter some aspersions on the propriety of his motives.

In Mr. Frye's behalf it is to be said that no man in high public life has borne a more untarnished reputation for probity than he. His period of service in Congress extends through nearly thirty years. With almost no elements of personal popularity, with a brusque, ill-natured manner that repels even his friends and admirers, it would be seemingly impossible for him to maintain his hold on the Republicans of Maine, were not unusual ability joined with high principle to make him a leader. His position in Maine may be compared to that of Hoar in Massachusetts, Cullom in Illinois, Allison in Iowa, or Hawley in Connecticut. Upright men are sometimes capable of very downright prejudices, and it is not necessary to attribute corrupt motives to Mr. Frye, as many Californians are disposed to do, to account for his determined advocacy of the railroad's interest. Once convinced, on the argument of the Southern Pacific engineers, that the Santa Monica site was the preferable one, Mr. Frye thenceforth would have regarded himself as a demagogue if he had listened for one moment to the demands of the people of Los Angeles that their harbor should be open to competition. We can readily understand his mental attitude, for it is one that is frequently assumed by Eastern peo-

SENATOR WM. B. FRYE of Maine.

ple who know California but distantly. All opposition to the railway, no matter what the merits of the particular case may be, is classed as agrarianism—any defense of the people's rights was demagogy, to Senator Frye. The demand for a "free harbor at San Pedro" reeked of Denis Kearney and the Sand Lots! And this one piece of prejudice working its way into a mind that was prompted both by experience and environment to accept it, operated as the elder Hamlet describes the poison

> " Swift as quicksilver it courses through
> The natural gates and alleys of the body,
> And with a sudden vigor it doth posset
> And curd, like eager droppings into milk,
> The thin and wholesome blood."

As to the first inception of this prejudice against Los Angeles and its harbor of San Pedro, it is not impossible that the incidents connected with his first visit to those localities may have a bearing upon it.

The party, which we have described, left the cars at the end of the Southern Pacific line, which then ran out to a spot beyond Timm's Point, where the company was engaged in building a new wharf of considerable length.

Dr. J. P. Widney, who was chairman of the committee of the Chamber of Commerce that had charge of the harbor work, and who had made a special study of the subject, unrolled a chart showing the proposed improvement, and started in to explain the plan, but Mr. Frye interrupted.

"Why, where are all the ships?" he said. "I was given to understand that there was something of a harbor here, and that a great deal of traffic was carried on, though under unfavorable conditions."

Major E. W. Jones, the president of the Chamber, replied that the best answer to the Senator's question would be found in the statistics of the port, which showed that it was entered by over 1000 vessels the preceding year, in spite of the neglect which it had suffered from the government, and the present unfavorable conditions for commerce.

Senator Frye then inspected the map. "Rattlesnake Island," he read aloud. "Deadman's Island. I should think it would scare a mariner to death to come into such a place."

"If that is all the difficulty," said Senator Stanford, evidently a little annoyed at the tone that Frye had adopted toward the party, "you let us have a large enough appropriation, and we will change the names to something less horrifying."

SOME JOCULAR REMARKS.

"Well, as near as I can make out," continued Mr. Frye, looking up from the map, "you propose to ask the government to create a harbor for you, almost out of whole cloth. The Lord has not given you much to start with, that is certain. It will cost four or five millions to build, you say; well, is your whole country worth that much?"

At this most unexpected utterance the Los Angeles delegation gazed at one another in astonishment and disgust, and they were relieved and gratified when Senator Stanford came to their aid, with a few words of description of the country, its existing resources and its splendid possibilities

MAJOR E. W. JONES.

under development. He also spoke of the opportunity which the favorable grades at this locality presented for trans-Pacific commerce.

"Well," said Mr. Frye, obstinately, in conclusion, "it seems that you have made a big mistake in the location of your city. You should have put it at some point where a harbor already exists, instead of calling upon the United States Government to give you what nature has refused."

"If we were to carry out that idea," said Senator Stanford, "we should have no cities on this coast for a space of 600 miles."

The party then returned to the city. The next day, when the Senator's remarks were published both in Los Angeles and San Diego, and considerable indignation was expressed among the citizens of the former city, he gave an interview to an evening paper, in which he said that his observations were intended to be of a jocular order, and should not be taken too seriously.*

Now, if Mr. Frye had remained an opponent of any appropriation for a harbor near Los Angeles, on the ground that it was not needed, he would have at least shown the virtue of consistency. A few years later, however, the extraordinary fact developed that while the Maine Senator could see no reason for spending any of the government money at San Pedro, he was warmly in favor of making an improvement at Santa Monica, in accordance with Mr. Huntington's ideas, which would cost about three millions of dollars.

It is perhaps needless to say, in concluding this chapter, that Mr. Frye does not enjoy a high degree of popularity in Southern California. Doubtless that is a matter of small moment to Mr. Frye; it is merely recorded here as a pertinent and perhaps an interesting piece of history.

---

* Senator Frye's own account of this incident given in his speech before the Senate May 11th, 1896, on the San Pedro-Santa Monica controversy is as follows:

Whether I am a "navigator" or not, I made my mind very deliberately then that a safe harbor at San Pedro was an impossibility, on account of the southeast winds. I so told Senator Stanford. He argued the question with me, and by that time there were a hundred or two hundred people around listening, and I finally, in jest, said to the Senator, "Senator, if those Los Angeles people want a harbor, suppose they move their city down to San Diego There is a good harbor there." You ought to have read the Los Angeles papers the next day. I never got such a lecture in my life as I got from those newspapers, and some of them have kept it up ever since.

CHAPTER VI.

The Government Considers the Outer Harbor.

IT was in the spring of 1890 that the first tangible result of the agitation in favor of the deep-water harbor was achieved. Through the efforts of Senator Stanford and Representative Vandever, an item was inserted in the River and Harbor appropriation bill, which passed in the summer of 1890, allowing the sum of $5000 to pay the expense of preparing a project for a deep-water harbor, somewhere in the vicinity of Los Angeles. The location was not described, except that it should be "between Points Dume and Capistrano." A Board of Engineers of the War Department was appointed, consisting of Col. G. H. Mendell, Lieut.-Col. G. L. Gillespie and Lieut.-Col. W. H. H. Benyaurd. Col. Mendell was the author of the two projects for the improvement of the inner harbor, which were then under way, and during a great part of that work, Lieut.-Col. W. H. H. Benyaurd was in charge. Both were therefore thoroughly familiar with the conditions that prevailed on the coast, and competent to render a decision as to the merits of the various localities.

It was subsequently urged by the advocates of the Santa Monica site against these gentlemen, that they were, in a way, already committed to the San Pedro site, having selected it twenty years before, as the proper place for government work, and that it would have been better, and more conducive to an impartial judgment, had the Secretary of War selected engineers from some distant section of the Union. On the other hand, it should be remembered that the question they were now called upon to consider was that of an outer harbor, and that they might with entire consistency have awarded that to some other spot than San Pedro—for the outer and inner harbor bore no direct relationship to one another, except that it would naturally be advantageous to have them both in the same vicinity, other things being equal.

The bill authorizing the appointment of this Board was

passed September 19, 1890, and the report was prepared during the following summer. The Board held public meetings in Santa Monica, San Pedro and Los Angeles, although there was no great amount of publicity given to the matter at the time. As every one supposed the location selected would be San Pedro, there was not much discussion and no excitement.

The report was submitted to Congress December 19th, 1891. The text of the law under which the Board was appointed is as follows:

> That the Secretary of War is authorized and directed to appoint a board of three engineer officers of the United States army, whose duty it shall be to examine the Pacific Coast between Points Dume and Capistrano, with a view to determining the best location for a deep-water harbor. The said board shall report to the Secretary of War a project for a deep-water harbor, with the estimated cost of the same, who shall lay said report before Congress at the next session, together with the views of the commission and of the Chief of Engineers of the United States army thereon; and the sum of five thousand dollars, or so much thereof as may be necessary, is hereby appropriated for the purpose.

The report, after giving a brief description of the topography of the region, disposes in a few words of all other harbor possibilities than San Pedro and Santa Monica, which latter are considered at some length. The following interesting and correct account is given of the winds of this coast:

> The prevailing wind on the California coast is from the northwest, nearly parallel to the coast line north of Point Concepcion, which is in latitude 34 deg., 27 min. At this point the trend of the coast changes from northwest to west. This fact, in connection with the bold topography of the shore, causes the prevailing winds along the southerly coast of California to be westerly. This wind never becomes more than a moderate gale. It never produces the heaviest waves. The disturbance of the water due to it is, however, always an inconvenience to vessels lying at a wharf exposed to its action, and when the disturbance is greatest there is danger to vessels. This wind prevails on the southern coast during the greater part of the year, with intermission of calms in the autumn and winter. In the last named season occur the

southerly offshore winds, which produce the heaviest waves to which the coast line is exposed.

A northeasterly land wind, known as the "Santa Ana," occasionally blows from the dry, hot plains lying to the eastward. Its duration is short, and it is severe, but having no fetch over the sea it raises no waves near the shore.

The southeaster comes in the winter and spring, and brings rain. The storm first manifests itself by a wind from the southeast, which continues for a few hours, shifting then to the south and southwest. The storm clears up when the wind gets to the northwest. In these storms a heavy sea is developed, which breaks upon the coast line in waves of great magnitude. These waves come from the south and southwest. The waves produced by the southeast wind are short, designated by the sailors as "choppy." The south and southwest seas, on the other hand, are long and heavy. A vessel at anchor under this exposure must, under these circumstances, get to sea with the possibility of otherwise going ashore. It is the heave of the sea rather than the wind, although the latter alone is sufficiently dangerous, that makes the strongest ground tackle, at times, of no avail.

Although southerly winds prevail during the winter seasons, and bring rain, yet their occurrence in violent form is not frequent, and a season has been known to pass without a severe storm. Nor is the duration of a storm rarely extended over two or three days.

In this respect the conditions of the southern coast of California are much less severe than in higher latitudes. This consideration is of great importance, for the reason that owing to it a lighter profile may be adopted for a breakwater than would be admissible much further north.

The structure proposed and considered for Santa Monica was to be placed directly in front of the city, instead of at Port Los Angeles, the location afterwards advocated by the railroad company. A breakwater thus situated, 8250 feet in length, would cover an anchorage ground, so the report states, between Point Dume and Rocky Point. The westerly 2000 feet would be in water of $7\frac{1}{2}$ to 9 fathoms, the remainder of the structure being 8 and 9 fathoms. It was estimated that this would cost, if built of rubble and concrete, $5,715,965, or of rubble only, $4,843,440.

The plan considered for San Pedro was somewhat different from the one finally adopted, eight years later. The report reads:

> In San Pedro Bay the best location for the proposed harbor is at the present anchorage ground on the west side of the bay under Point Fermin. The projection of the westerly shore, by which protection is afforded from westerly winds, and from which a breakwater could start, affords advantages over any other section of the bay to the eastward for securing a protected anchorage.
>
> Good holding ground exists at the anchorage. Protection from storms over the open arcs of exposure to the southwest and southeast could be secured by the construction of a breakwater having two arms. Catalina affords protection from southwest seas as before stated, over an angle of forty-eight degrees. The westerly arm could be started from a point on the shore under Point Fermin, and be extended in a direction south 41 degrees east (magnetic), for a distance of about 2,400 feet, which would carry it beyond a line projected from the middle of the present anchorage ground to the westerly end of Catalina Island. The end of this arm is in six fathoms depth. Then leaving a gap of 1,500 feet, the easterly arm could be given a direction north 56½ degrees east, along the 9½ fathom curve, and be extended about 5,600 feet, which would afford protection from the southeast seas. This arm could be extended easterly as increased commerce would require more interior space.

The estimated cost of this structure, if built of rubble and concrete, was $4,594,494; if built entirely of concrete, the cost was figured at $4,126,106.

The report then goes into a comparison of the two locations, showing the superiority of San Pedro on every point, Its final summing up of the case reads as follows:

> In view of the fact that San Pedro Bay in its natural condition affords better protection both from prevailing winds and from dangerous storms than Santa Monica Bay;
>
> That protection can be secured at less cost for equal development of breakwater at the former than at the latter;
>
> That a larger area of protected anchorage from the prevailing westerly swells can be secured, the severe storms from the southwest being infrequent;
>
> And that there is already an interior harbor that will be a valuable addition to the outer harbor;

A MEMORIAL TO CONGRESS.

} The Board considers San Pedro Bay as the better location for the deep-water harbor provided for by the act.

When this document was made public, its immediate effect was to quiet whatever doubt may have existed as to the exact spot where the deep-water harbor was to be constructed, and to give the advocates of that improvement fresh strength and courage. The Chamber of Commerce prepared a new memorial, asking that the work to be undertaken forthwith, and sent a copy to every member of Congress. This memorial bears the names of H. Z. Osborne, who was then serving as Collector of the Port, Henry T. Hazard, Mayor of Los Angeles, W. H. Workman, ex-mayor and

HENRY T. HAZARD.

an old-time harbor advocate, Hervey Lindley, who ran for Congress the next year on the Republican ticket and was defeated, and James Cuzner, of the lumber firm of Kerckhoff & Cuzner. Of these H. Z. Osborne and Hervey Lindley afterward became active Santa Monica advocates.

In order to assist Mr. Bowers, who served as Representative, 1891-93, in securing an appropriation, the Chamber of Commerce sent on a special delegate in the person of General Lionel A. Sheldon, a former Member of Congress from Louisiana.* But the conditions were unfavorable, and nothing could be accomplished.

In the meantime an important change had taken place in the personnel of the management of the Southern Pacific railroad. Senator Leland Stanford, who had acted as president of the Central Pacific since its beginning, and who, when that road was merged into the Southern Pacific, became the president of the whole system, was suddenly and unexpectedly deposed, and Mr. C. P. Huntington took his place. The dramatic character of the proceedings at the annual meeting, where the change occurred, produced a great sensation all over the State.

For many years elections of officers and directors in the Southern Pacific Company had been of a perfunctory and commonplace character, and there was beforehand no outward indication that the meeting of April 9th, 1890, would differ in any wise from those that had immediately preceded it. But when the vote of the stockholders was taken, it developed that the Hopkins interest, which had formerly been in alliance with the Crocker and Stanford interests, had changed over to Huntington, and that the latter was now completely in control.

There had been for some time rumors of strained relations between Stanford and Huntington, due partly to a disagreement with regard to the management of the road, and partly to certain complications of a social character that had arisen in the two families. The public was, however, considerably astonished when C. P. Huntington, immediately upon his election to the presidency of the road, read to the stockholders a typewritten address, which he afterwards handed to the reporters, in which he deliberately insulted and denounced Mr. Stanford. Incidents of that character sometimes occur behind closed doors of corporation offices, over the long green table in the directors' room, but it is a little unusual to have them develop in the broad daylight of newspaper publicity.

---

* By a curious coincidence it was General Sheldon who, as a member of the House Committee dealing with River and Harbor appropriations nearly twenty years before, had assisted Colonel Houghton in getting the first appropriation for San Pedro.

"At all times," said Mr. Huntington, reading aloud from his address, "my personal interest has been second to that of the company; and in no case will I use this great corporation to advance my personal ambition at the expense of the owners, or put my hands into its treasury to defeat the people's choice, and thereby put myself in positions that should be filled by others; but to the best of my ability will I work for the interest of the stockholders of this company and the people whom it should serve."

No other construction could be put upon this utterance

LELAND STANFORD.

than that it pointed directly at Mr. Stanford, who, while president of the company, was twice honored by election to the Senatorship. The phrase "put myself in positions that should be filled by others" was supposed to refer to ex-Senator Sargent, who was dropped to make room for Stanford. If there was need, however, that any one should be "edified by the margent" as to Mr. Huntington's meaning, his own subsequent interviews in the San Francisco dailies, which were full of bitterness against Mr. Stanford, made it perfectly clear.

The new president then proceeded to deliver some very proper sentiments on the duty of corporations and their employees, which read somewhat strangely now at the end of nine years of the administration of Mr. Huntington.

"The best results cannot be brought about unless every officer of the company gives his best attention to the care of the company's interests, which can be best done without interfering in political affairs. The people are everywhere jealous of great corporations. Let us conduct this company so that all good people will be with us. If this is not done, your president will certainly be on the side of the people. Corporations should not be used to advance the interests of this party or that, or to raise up any one man or to pull down another; and this corporation will not be so used henceforth, if its president can prevent it."

This portion of the address was received with a good deal of derision by the people of California, for it was Mr. Huntington himself that had always managed the company's political work in Washington and at Sacramento, and there was extant a very interesting bundle of letters, written by him to one of his fellow directors of the company, General Colton, in which he had described in detail his dubious methods in the lobby, with the utmost sang froid.

However, the matter of Mr. Huntington's sincerity or his fitness for the utterance of such sentiments is not part of the present discussion. The point to be noted, as bearing on the San Pedro issue, is that the new head of the road came to his work imbued with the idea that his predecessor had mismanaged the property. It was announced on all sides that there was to be a "new deal," a "general shaking up" and certain radical changes of policy, and there certainly was warrant for this assumption in the way Mr. Huntington expressed himself, as he went about inspecting the road. He visited San Pedro and Santa Monica, and announced that the company would soon make some important improvements in the latter locality.

Presently the work which was in progress at San Pedro on the wharf near Timm's Point came to a halt. No public statement of any kind was made on the subject until, five years later, when the harbor discussion was at its liveliest, Mr. Wm. Hood, the head of the engineering department of the road, declared that the great difficulty which was experienced in driving the piles of the wharf on account of the rocky bottom, had caused the abandonment of the undertaking.

Within a few months after Mr. Huntington became president of the Southern Pacific, work began on the construction of the line from Santa Monica to Port Los Angeles, and a year later that line was in operation and work on the long wharf was well under way. In 1893 the wharf was completed, and the Southern Pacific was committed to the change of policy from a harbor at San Pedro to one at Santa Monica. As the reasons for this change lie within the controversial limits, they should be given in detail, both from the railroad's point of view and from that of its opponents; and a new chapter must be opened for their benefit.

CHAPTER VII.

THE SOUTHERN PACIFIC'S CHANGE OF BASE.

THE first formal announcement of the decision of the railroad company to abandon San Pedro and take up Santa Monica was made in February, 1892, in a telegram from Wm. Hood, the chief engineer of the Southern Pacific, to Senator Frye, which was presented to the Senate Committee on Commerce. In this telegram Mr. Hood warned the committee, which was at that time considering the advisability of making an appropriation for San Pedro, in accordance with the project of the Mendell Board, that the holding ground at San Pedro was rocky and not usable, and that the railroad company had encountered such difficulty in driving piles for the construction of a wharf in the outer harbor area that it had been compelled to give up the work, and was now putting in a pier at Santa Monica instead.

It is probable that the decision to go to Santa Monica was reached by Mr. Huntington some time in 1891.

Santa Monica is a town of about 3000 population situated on the coast directly west of Los Angeles, and possessing superior advantages as a beach resort. It has been

RESIDENCE OF SENATOR JONES AT SANTA MONICA, CAL.

for half a century or more the favorite summer watering place for the people of Los Angeles and the interior towns, and although at present it has active rivals in Long Beach, Catalina, Terminal Island and Redondo, it still gathers by far the greater number of summer visitors.

In 1875 Senator John P. Jones of Nevada and several Los Angeles capitalists, of whom J. S. Slauson was the chief, undertook to make Santa Monica a commercial port. They constructed a railroad from that place to the city, and put out a wharf 1,800 feet in length for the accommodation of such traffic as could be secured, more particularly for the use of the Pacific Coast Steamship Company. The charges exacted by the Southern Pacific on its line from San Pedro to Los Angeles were regarded by the people of Southern California as outrageously exorbitant—$2.50 for carrying a passenger, and freight at five to ten times its present figure. The Santa Monica railroad and wharf were therefore hailed as a deliverance from a monopoly, and for a short period there was active competition. At the end of a year and a half, however, the Los Angeles investors found that they were not receiving the support from the people to which they considered they had a just title, and when the opportunity occurred to part with the property to advantage they embraced it, and the road and wharf passed into the hands of the Southern Pacific. The general community was permanently benefited to a considerable degree, as the old rates were not restored, even though competition had ceased.

Mr. J. S. Slauson was, through the whole of the subsequent harbor controversy, an ardent advocate of Santa Monica, basing his predeliction for that port on his ancient experience. He is now (1899) president of the Chamber of Commerce of Los Angeles.

For a few years the Southern Pacific made use of the wharf at Santa Monica, but in the later '70s they abandoned it, and tore down the outer end of the structure, declaring that it was unsafe even for foot passengers. Their reasons for leaving Santa Monica at this time, as set forth by Mr. Hood, in his testimony before the Craighill Board—fifteen years later—were that vessels moored to the wharf, even in comparatively good weather, suffered so from the swell that the Pacific Coast Steamship Company, its principal user, at last refused to guarantee to come to a landing there. This evidence was given, it must be noted, after the railway company had changed back again to Santa Monica though to a somewhat different location—and hence, doubtless, puts the case rather mildly.

In those days, as at present, a very large percentage—nearly all, in fact—of the freight and passenger business for Los Angeles came from the north, and it probably occurred to the builders of the original Santa Monica line that their port, being twenty-five miles nearer San Francisco than is San Pedro, and also three or four miles nearer Los Angeles, would naturally take away from the ancient embarcadero all the freight and passenger business that could be conveniently handled through Santa Monica. It was in pursuance of this same theory that in the year 1889, the Redondo Railway Company, an organization of capitalists from Oregon, whose leaders, Captains Ainsworth and Thompson, had enjoyed large experience in coast transportation, constructed a wharf at Redondo and a narrow gauge railway to Los Angeles from that point. Redondo is on the southern corner of Santa Monica Bay, just about midway between Santa Monica and San Pedro. Owing to the existence of a submarine canyon directly in front of the town, it was possible to reach deep water with a short wharf, and the topography of the shore was such as to give a safe anchorage for deep-sea vessels, except on the rare occasions when great storms prevailed. Within a year after the Redondo company had blazed the way, the Santa Fe followed; and a second wharf was constructed at Redondo; and presently great quantities of freight from the north began to flow into Los Angeles by way of the new port. In 1890 182 vessels landed cargoes there; in 1891, 194; and in 1892, 250. Among these were many deep-sea vessels that had formerly been compelled to make use of the slow and expensive method of delivering their cargoes by lighters at San Pedro; and some of them came from New York by way of Cape Horn.

By the year 1892 it was computed that over 60 per cent of all the water traffic in and out of Los Angeles, if coal and lumber were excluded, was passing by way of Redondo.

Now, the coal that came into San Pedro was largely used by the Southern Pacific, hence the company was limited to its lumber business and about half its former general merchandise business to pay expenses and profits on its San Pedro branch; and from being a very handsome piece of property that line began to hang a dead weight.

There was still one more element of disadvantage in the Southern Pacific's San Pedro location, and one which is rated by many people as most serious, although it was made light of by the officials of the road, and that was the entrance of the Terminal Railway into good wharfage ground on the east side of the interior harbor. The Terminal Company was a corporation formed for the purpose of acquiring and holding terminal facilities in the city of Los Angeles and upon the ocean front, with a view to subsequently leasing them to larger systems of railways. At the time the road was built which was in 1891-2, it was generally understood that the Union Pacific, which was just then undergoing reorganization, and was attempting new development, or perhaps some one of the other roads that were working their way westward from Denver, would come down from Salt Lake over the easy grades of Utah, Nevada and the California desert country, to Los Angeles, and that the Terminal was to be its Los Angeles and deep-water outlet. The approach of the panic deferred immediate action, and then followed the long era of bad times, so that even at this writing, the expected connection with Salt Lake City has not been achieved. Undoubtedly the projectors of the Terminal, who are capitalists and railway builders living in St. Louis, R. C. Kerens and Geo. B. Leighton among them, are in touch with any development that is likely to come to Los Angeles from a northwesterly direction, and it is proper enough even yet to refer to the Terminal as the probable last link of a new transcontinental line. It was in that form that it originally appeared in the section, and the regard in which it was held by the people was in some measure affected by their gratification over this promise of new gain in railway strength.

In establishing its connections to the north and northeast from Los Angeles—to Glendale and to Pasadena—the Terminal purchased existing motor roads, but when it made its way to the sea it constructed a new and an independent line. Relying upon the judgment of the United States engineers, that San Pedro was the proper place for a deep-sea harbor to be located, in the event that the government should decide to build one, and believing that Congress must of necessity follow the advice of the engineers, the new company chose San Pedro as its ocean terminus. Its line parallels the Southern Pacific about five miles further to the east, until it reaches Long Beach; thence it makes its way along the coast over Rattlesnake—or, as it was rechristened, Terminal Island—to East San Pedro. On the western shore of the island, along the interior harbor, wharves were constructed and lumber, coal and miscellaneous merchandise from the sea began to come in by this route.

Thus it is shown that the Southern Pacific, regarding the matter purely from a business standpoint, had ample justification for its efforts to secure a new landing place, and it chose—as was most natural—the point that was farthest to the north and was yet practicable for use, and also the location where it was least likely to be annoyed by competitors. The spot selected was at Port Los Angeles— the name given it by Mr. John M. Crawley, the Los Angeles agent of the Southern Pacific—about two miles north of Santa Monica and half a mile north of the mouth of Santa Monica canyon.

The railway line to Santa Monica was extended by means of a tunnel and cut through the bluff, which brought the road out on the ocean front. The beach at this point is a little over 300 feet wide and the bluff is about 70 feet high. As the road continues to the north, the bluff increases in height, until 180 feet is reached in the vicinity of the wharf. The width of the beach is about the same throughout, the distance varying, we may say, from 300 to 400 feet.

The wharf which the company put out at this spot may be perhaps best described by reproducing an official utterance—a clause in the report of the board of 1896—the last of the many harbor commissions

"The pier built by the Southern Pacific is a very thoroughly constructed timber pier, the piles being creosoted and the superstructure carefully designed. In locating the pier care was taken to align it as nearly as possible in the direction of the approach of the heaviest swells, which was determined experimentally to be south 42 degrees 24 minutes west, magnetic. The tracks of the Southern Pacific railway run to the extreme end of this pier, around which is a well-arranged system of mooring buoys, so that vessels lying at the pier can be breasted off, leaving them free to rise and fall with the swell. The pier is 4,300 feet long and terminates in 5½ fathoms of water. It is the most carefully designed and thoroughly constructed ocean pier on the California coast."

Its cost was on one occasion stated by Mr. Huntington to be about $1,000,000. This was the figure which Mr. Frye used several times when he referred to it in the Senate and in committee. It is quite probable that Mr. Huntington did not mean the wharf alone, but included in the sum which he mentioned, the line to the wharf and other contingent improvements. Its actual cost was somewhere in the neighborhood of $600,000.

The best authority as to the views and purposes of the Southern Pacific road in this whole matter, outside of Mr. Huntington himself—and perhaps in some ways a better authority even than Mr. Huntington—is Mr. Hood. The head of the engineering department of a great railway system like the Southern Pacific is something more than an engineer. He is of necessity a financier, a business man, a lawyer, a manager of men and a diplomat. He is, or should be, an "all round" man, as the every-day phrase expresses it; and Mr. Hood comes very near filling this difficult and extensive bill of particulars. His management of the Southern Pacific's case for Santa Monica, through two successive investigations by government boards, was worthy of the praise that it received even from the opponents of that side; and the defeat which he met in each case, and the ultimate failure of his cause, was certainly not due to any lack of judgment on his part, but to the difficult policy he was called upon to support. It is, by the way, one splendidly redeeming quality of this corporation, that it attracts to its service so many men of fine character and exceptional abilities, who never waver in their allegiance, and who, even under the most trying circumstances, will maintain at once their devotion to the road, their own self-respect and the ardent regard of those with whom they are in daily contact. It happened that the two men who were in charge of the Southern Pacific's affairs in Los Angeles, through the whole of this contest, Mr. John A. Muir, the superintendent of this division, and Mr. J. M. Crawley, the general agent, were men of this sort. They were good fighters, and they stood by the works as long as there was anything left to fight for; but they descended to nothing that was mean or tricky, they

JOHN M. CRAWLEY.

kept their tempers and accumulated no crop of private enemies—which makes up a record that may give them just pride.

But to return to Mr. Hood. When he was on the stand as a witness before the board of '92, he was asked why the Southern Pacific had given up its deep-water wharf project at San Pedro, and had entered upon one at Santa Monica. His answer—which is important as the statement of the railway side of the question—ran as follows: "In reference to Santa Monica, I will say that the Southern Pacific is a corporation that has many millions of dollars at stake in its business. It is not accustomed to build wharves 4,500 feet long, the length of which is for shipping facilities, when it already has such facilities at San Pedro. But it has been borne in on this company so peremptorily by nature—for freight and passenger business follows the laws of nature—that any company that relied wholly for their connection of rail with ships on San Pedro would go to the wall in that regard. So that now we are building, without any reference to any breakwater proposition, or deep-sea harbor proposition whatever, a wharf at Santa Monica which will, ten months in the year, take safely, we think, any sea-going vessels that choose to come there. We are going to carry that to completion, and the expense will be very great; there is where we expect to do a great deal of business. And it is so obvious to any business man that a company like the Southern Pacific is not going to make such an expenditure for any other reason than the actual necessities of the case, that I think it calls for no demonstration."

The primary reason, then, for the Southern Pacific's change of base from San Pedro to Santa Monica, according to the statement of one of its leading officials, was to secure the coast business which was slipping away from it. Subsequently various other reasons were developed; one was that the holding-ground at San Pedro was bad, but this was abandoned when put to the test; another was that the proposed deep-water harbor at San Pedro would be less adapted to any scheme of bringing ship and rail together than at Santa Monica, and that vessels lying at the former harbor were more subject to danger from winds and heavy seas than at the latter. In the end the road succeeded in working up a complete and well-rounded case against San Pedro and in favor of Santa Monica, based on purely technical grounds; but its action in the first place was undoubtedly from the motive of business interest alone.

CHAPTER VIII.

THE ISSUE TAKES SHAPE.

IN presenting the motives of the Southern Pacific's change of base, we have been compelled to anticipate, to some extent, the succession of events as they actually occurred. For example, it was not evident, at the time the long wharf at Santa Monica was begun in 1891, that the road contemplated any change in its attitude with reference to a deep-sea harbor. Indeed, it was not until the Craighill board met in the fall of 1892, that the outlines of the plan were developed, and even then the great majority of the people of Los Angeles were not disposed to regard the matter seriously. It was still another year before the nature of the entire scheme was reached, and the public came thoroughly to understand the issue and prepared to act upon it.

In the fall of 1891 Charles Felton, who had been appointed by the Governor to fill out the unexpired Senatorial term of George Hearst, deceased, visited Los Angeles on the request of the Chamber of Commerce, inspected the harbor at San Pedro, and was present at a public meeting when the matter of an appropriation to begin work on the outside harbor was discussed. General Vandever, whose four years of service as representative of the Sixth Congressional district had now concluded, and W. W. Bowers, of San Diego, his successor, were both present at this gathering. Mr. Felton inquired very thoroughly into the facts of the case, and promised to make it one of the special objects of his first year's work to secure the initial appropriation.

Early in 1892 Senator Felton and Representative Bowers wrote to the chamber, advising that, if possible, a special delegate be sent on to watch the San Pedro item in its progress through the two houses. This was in accordance with the plan already adopted by the chamber, and steadily adhered to ever since, of sending some capable representative citizen to assist the congressmen in caring for the section's commercial interest. This method was preferred to that in vogue in some quarters of hiring the expert, but often unscrupulous, lobbyists that may be had in Washington.

For this purpose the Chamber selected one of its directors, Mr. Charles Forman, a gentleman who is held in great esteem in Los Angeles for ability and high character. He has since that time served two terms as president of the organization, of which he was then a director. He was to be accompanied by a young man whose name will appear frequently in these pages hereafter, as a large factor in the

T. E. GIBBON.

fight, and, both for the part he played and for the unusual character that he is, he deserves more than passing mention.

Thomas Edward Gibbon, whose direct interest in the contest grows out of his position as attorney and vice-president of the Terminal railway, was at this time barely thirty years of age, and a comparatively recent accession to Los Angeles from Arkansas. The son of a studious and thoughtful country doctor, whose fortunes were broken by the war, but whose "library was dukedom large enough," he came through heredity to those scholarly characteristics that are to most men the outgrowth of years of work at school and college—representing privileges to him denied. After a youth spent in the hard, steady labor of the farm, with evenings of Shakespeare and Scott, he studied law, and began to practice in the city of Little Rock.

Politics was to him an infantile disease, from which he suffered acutely for a time, and then recovered, with no serious after-consequences. He was the youngest member of the Arkansas Legislature of 1895, and that the entire State was not reformed and made over forthwith was probably not due to any lack of enthusiasm and vigor on his part. The total collapse of his health, a year or two later, caused him to lay down his work and spend some months in Europe. Like three men out of four now living in Los Angeles, he came to Southern California "on a doctor's certificate." There he renewed the practice of law and the affairs of the Terminal were presently placed in his hands.

While Mr. Gibbon's part in the contest was affected to some extent, without doubt, by his relations to the Terminal, yet anyone who knows him well will admit that he must, sooner or later, have taken an active hand in the contest, had he been free from business affiliations with either side. In the first place, he inherits from some Irish ancestor that peculiarly delicate and indefinable characteristic which prompts men who are entirely averse to seeking a quarrel, thoroughly to enjoy one that is forced upon them. Then, again, being himself essentially a man of the people, and naturally democratic in his tastes and tendencies, Mr. Gibbon must inevitably have lined up with the anti-monopoly side of the fight. His heart was very thoroughly with his head in the battle, and a boundless enthusiasm, and a confidence in the ultimate success of what he believed to be the righteous cause, came to aid his indomitable perseverance and energy.

Mr. Gibbon was almost the first, if not indeed the very first, out of the many who were interested in the harbor at San Pedro, to outline the plan of the Southern Pacific to go to Santa Monica, abandoning the ancient harbor. Before his departure for Washington, in January of 1892, he detailed to one of the officers of the Chamber his theory that, owing to the gain in time between San Francisco and Santa Monica, as against San Pedro, the Southern Pacific was likely to favor the more northern port.

His theory did not receive much attention, but was attributed to the fact that he was a "new-comer" and presumably unacquainted with existing conditions. The Southern Pacific had for twenty years worked faithfully in conjunction with the people of Los Angeles for the development of San Pedro harbor, and they had even torn down and cut to pieces their wharf at Santa Monica. On the occasion of Senator Felton's recent visit to the port, the Southern Pacific had graciously provided a train free of charge for him and the Chamber of Commerce party. The corporation was a good friend of the people of this section; there was no such feeling against it as existed in the northern part of the State. Besides, to settle the question of location, once and for all, had not the government sent a commission of engineers, and had they not reported favorably on a harbor at San Pedro?

Circumstances delayed the departure of General Forman, and the bill coming on for early action in the Senate, it was not until the succeeding year that he fulfilled the mission. Mr. Gibbon went on alone, and presently returned with surprising news that confirmed his predictions.

True to his pledge Senator Felton had presented the cause of the San Pedro deep-water improvement so forcibly to the Committee on Commerce, that there seemed at one time a possibility that the item of $250,000, which was the sum set for the original direct appropriation, might carry.*

Then it was that Senator Frye produced a telegram signed by Wm. Hood, the Southern Pacific chief of engineers, which was the opening gun of the great contest.

It is to be regretted that no copy of this telegram forms part of the public record of the case, inasmuch as its exact substance was the cause of no little debate a few years later. It was asserted at the time, by those who heard it read, that it was chiefly taken up with the statement that the holding

---

* It was thought best not to attempt the continuing contract form of appropriation, but to apply for a portion of the required sum to be available directly.

ground at San Pedro was rock, and could not be made usable, and that the Southern Pacific's abandonment of its projected wharf to deep water at that place was due to the impossibility of driving piles into the hard bottom. Senator Frye evidently considered that the basis of the technical objection to San Pedro, for he referred to it time and again in his speeches, even after the Craighill board had thoroughly disproved the statement; and he quoted Mr. Hood as his authority. The interesting, not to say amusing, feature of the case, and the reason why the substance of the telegram was subsequently under dispute, was that four years later Mr. Hood testified before the Walker board that the holding ground of San Pedro was all right, and practically free from rock Of course, as a scientific man and as an engineer, he could not say anything else; for it is not a rocky bottom.

However, Mr. Hood's objections to San Pedro, as set forth in the famous mislaid telegram, were of a sort to prove convincing to the commerce committee, and the item of $250,000 was thrown out. Senator Felton then appealed to the committee to take the proper steps to settle the question of the harbor site—"once and for all"—and also, since the question had been asked by several members of the committee, whether there was any reason for building such a harbor at either location, to get a decision for that point as well.

In response to Senator Felton's appeal, the following was inserted in the River and Harbor bill of 1892, which formed the basis of the appointment of what was subsequently known as the "Craighill Board:"

> The Secretary of War is hereby authorized and directed to appoint a board of five engineering officers of the United States Army, whose duty it shall be to make a careful and critical examination for a proposed deep-water harbor at San Pedro or Santa Monica Bays, and to report which is the more eligible location for such a harbor in depth, width and capacity to accommodate the largest ocean-going vessels, and the commercial and naval necessities of the country, togther with an estimate of the cost of the same. Said Board of Engineers shall report the result of its investigations to the Secretary of War on or before the first of No-

vember, 1892; and ten thousand dollars, or so much thereof as may be necessary, are hereby apprpriated for said purpose.

The phrase "and the commercial and naval necessities of the country" was interpreted to mean that the Board should consider what relation the proposed harbor bore to the commerce not of Southern California alone but of the whole country. In this way the vexed question of whether any harbor was needed would also be settled "once and for all." The phrase is quoted because it at last became a byword with the people of Los Angeles, who saw one "final settlement" after another brushed aside by the Southern Pacific.

No one thought of Santa Monica as an alternative factor in the case, until the Craighill Board was about to begin its investigations the following summer, and the Southern Pacific formally took up the cause of Port Los Angeles. From this "no one," however, we must except Mr. Gibbon, and a few who had begun to listen with interest and some degree of confidence to the "damnable iteration" of his theories.

But even as people, one by one and slowly, came to understand the Southern Pacific's position, there was no feeling of special resentment against that corporation since its right to favor any locality it might choose for such an improvement was generally conceded. Many regretted that the issue had been raised, but they made no question that the board which was to be appointed would put an end to all debate.

The citizens of Los Angeles and vicinity were at that time generally well-disposed toward the Southern Pacific; it had treated the people fairly and had received full justice in return. There were not lacking, of course, those who made a point of explaining that this amicable state of affairs was entirely due to the presence in Southern California of an active competitor, and that in the northern part of the State—where no such competition existed—the Southern Pacific was in very bad odor for its exactions and its harsh treatment of patrons; but to them it was answered that the north might fight its own battles: we of the south were not concerned. The general sentiment with regard to the railroad was that it had been one of the most important factors in bringing prosperity to the section, fighting its way across the desert country of the southwest, at a time when the outlook was most discouraging, and opening up with its many branches all sections of Southern California. It was operated in a thorough, systematic and orderly style, which at that time presented something of a contrast to its chief competitor, the Santa Fe, then in the depths of financial difficulty.* Its people were trained to politeness and consideration, and they were, as a rule, well liked. It rarely happens that a railway corporation, as such, can be described as popular, especially in a country where, according to Poor's Manual, more than half of the securities for which earnings must be made are fictitious; nevertheless, the Southern Pacific in Los Angeles up to and even into the beginning of the harbor contest, came very near to enjoying that exalted state.

Therefore it happened, that when the purposes of the road were finally developed, a great many people, who had been warm advocates of the San Pedro location, began to declare openly, that if our great and good friend Huntington—great for his wealth and his recognized power at Washington, and good in that he seemed to favor us as against the northern part of the State—desired the harbor to go to Santa Monica, he should be given his own way—what difference did it make to the people of Los Angeles? Santa Monica was several miles nearer than San Pedro. It was a beautiful location and popular as a summer resort, while there were drunken sailors frequently to be seen at the other place. Probably the government engineers had made some mistake; Mr. Hood was a high authority in the profession.

To this an answer was offered, that Congress was not likely to appropriate money for a harbor against the advice of its own engineers; and it was also stated, now for the first time, that the Southern Pacific had been buying land along the shore where the proposed harbor was to be located, and if Santa Monica won, it meant a "monopoly harbor."

However, before the debate had more than fairly begun, the

---

* This condition of contrast, it is perhaps needless to say, no longer exists, for the Santa Fé at the present time is one of the best equipped and best conducted roads in the Union.

Craighill Board came to Los Angeles, and a general armistice was decreed until their report should be heard. On all hands it was admitted that this report was to "settle the question."

CHAPTER IX.
THE CRAIGHILL BOARD.

THE Board of Engineers, which Senator Felton's amendment called for, was appointed early in July, 1892, and consisted of the following: Colonel Wm. P. Craighill, Lieutenant-Colonel Henry M. Robert, Lieutenant-Colonel Peter C. Hains, Major C. W. Raymond and Major Thos. H. Handbury, all of the United States corps of engineers, and well skilled in harbor work.

This Board convened at San Francisco in September, and after examining the maps and charts on file at headquarters of the Coast and Geodetic survey, repaired to Los Angeles, where it was announced they would hold a public meeting on the 8th at the rooms of the Chamber of Commerce.

Some little surprise was expressed at the idea of a public meeting for the consideration of what was supposed to be purely a technical issue, but subsequent developments proved the wisdom of this plan. While it is not probable that any very material facts that assisted the Board in coming to a decision, were brought out by this process, it did away with the possibility of any claim that the proceedings were of a "star chamber" character, or that either side failed of a fair hearing. It is the established practice of the government in such cases to call on the people generally for any evidence they may have to offer; and afterward a technical consideration is given to winds, waves, currents, soundings, borings, and other matters on which the public is presumably not so well informed.

The Chamber of Commerce tendered its large meeting hall for the use of the Board, its officers stating that while the organization had heretofore been in favor of the San Pedro location, now that the question was opened up afresh by the government, it would maintain an attitude of neutrality.

Several hundred people were present at the meeting, about equally divided in number between the three ports of San Pedro, Santa Monica and Redondo. C. M. Wells, the president of the Chamber, occupied the chair, and in his opening remarks said:

> It is proper to say that, in this matter of selecting the best site for a harbor upon this coast, the Chamber of Commerce is not taking a part; is not throwing its influence in favor of one place as against another. Los Angeles city and the surrounding country desire a deep-water harbor, and we all understand that it is the effort of these eminent engineering officers to determine which is the most suitable point for the construction of such a harbor, and where it can be constructed at the least cost. So that the Chamber of Commerce is simply aiding these engineers in collecting their information; and that is what this meeting is for.

Although a large part of the testimony offered was of an irregular and unscientific character — as was to be expected — and some of it partook rather of the nature of stump speaking, a number of points were brought out that had a decided bearing on the contest, whatever weight they may have had with the engineers.

The question of the Southern Pacific ownership in and around the Santa Monica location was thus briefly touched upon by Mr. Shorb in his opening remarks:

> There are some matters that I think ought to be given public expression to here. I do not speak with any rancor or any unkindness, but there are some things that look rather peculiar, and that we, as citizens, have a right to inquire into. During all these years, since Alexander and Mendell and those gentlemen have been employed in completing the improvements at San Pedro, the advantages there have principally been to the Southern Pacific Company. I have had long conversations with Governor Stanford and Mr. Huntington. Both these gentlemen have time and again said that Wilmington was their only point. Governor Stanford told me himself that he proposed to make it the work of his senatorial life to secure for that point such appropriations as might be needed. He even went so far, after acquiring wharf privileges at Santa

Monica and building and using a wharf, as to pull it down. I think it is a privilege and a right for us to enquire now: How is it that those gentlemen think all that has been done down here has been wasted money, and that the only point for the government engineers to select is some place down here in the gorge of Santa Monica, which, according to common report—I don't state it as a fact, and I have no doubt that these gentlemen will answer that proposition—is to work to their exclusive advantage, if built?

The same point was argued more at length by Dr. J. P. Widney, as follows:

I went with Governor Stanford over the San Pedro harbor several times. For twelve or fifteen years they said only one thing: "There is no other point on this coast where we have even thought of going." And they examined it all carefully. And Governor Stanford said: "I expect to live to see the day when our commerce goes to San Pedro instead of San Francisco." And they stayed there for years. And that was their only point when they tore down their wharf at Santa Monica, and said that it was worthless. Now they want to change front and say, "We will go to Santa Monica." I am sorry to say, gentlemen, we have realized one thing in this country. The Southern Pacific came here and at first had everybody for its friend; but we have learned that when they want anything very badly our interest lies the other way. They have whirled front, after about fifteen years use and advocacy of San Pedro, and have gone to Santa Monica and are building a wharf there. And I would advise our citizens to ask who owns the land right back of there. I don't know. I know some of my acquaintances were endeavoring to buy a certain tract of land down about Santa Monica canyon, involving a great many hundred acres. The man said it was bid in for the Southern Pacific. It is gone. We have lost it. It is not in their name, but it is bought for them. Here is a narrow strip of land in front of a bluff about one hundred feet high, and the Southern Pacific has a right-of-way all along that; and that is where the breakwater is to go; and what chance has anybody else? At San Pedro we have two railroads in already. We have a large private ownership on the interior harbor, and the city retains part ownership.

The Southern Pacific answer to these "miserable insinuations," as they were denominated by Judge Carpenter, who conducted the case for that corporation and for Santa Monica, was to place on the stand Mr. Chas. Monroe, an attorney of Los Angeles, who testified that as the representatives of Messrs. Jones and Baker, who owned the land along the beach from the town of Santa Monica to the canyon, he had arranged the papers for the right-of-way of the Southern Pacific, giving them a strip 50 feet wide directly under the bluff, and that the object of Messrs. Jones and Baker in so placing the right-of-way had been to leave room for other railroads between the Southern Pacific and tide water; and also Mr. Wm. Hood, who showed a plat of the property holdings along the beach in the vicinity of the proposed breakwater. He stated that a gentleman, who might be regarded as the representative of Mr. C. P. Huntington, held 2,000 feet of frontage running to the water's edge immediately back of the wharf, but he declared that this left over two-thirds of the protected area still open to use by other roads. In the cross-examination by Mr. Gibbon the situation was developed somewhat further, as follows:

Mr. Gibbon: As I understand you, this land here, extending from the canyon, is the private property of Mr. Huntington, the president of the company?

Mr. Hood: I say it is my opinion that it is. I don't know the details, but I understand it to be so; and you might as well assume it.

Mr. Gibbon: That is land with a very high bluff?

Mr. Hood: Yes, sir.

Mr. Gibbon: And your company owns or controls all this property here. That represents a frontage of how much?

Mr. Hood: It is about 2000 feet, more or less.

Mr. Gibbon: What we are getting at just now is the length of the usable land for railroad purposes, the breadth, rather, between those aligning bluffs and tide water.

Mr. Hood: I think other roads could go parallel with ours, outside the right of way, for about seventy-five or eighty feet, and hold it, as we propose to hold it, with rock.

Mr. Gibbon: But you cut off all access here. It is necessary to cut across your track to get across here.

Mr. Hood: It would be; but there is room here.

Mr. Gibbon: In point of fact, your company at the

present time occupies a strip of land the full width of the water front, leaving possible for any other company a very narrow strip of, say, seventy-five feet in width?

Mr. Hood: No, averaging at least a hundred; about room for seven tracks, without doing any strengthening work to protect against the ocean.

Mr. Gibbon: And there is no possible approach from this side, because that is all bluff?

Mr. Hood: That would be very difficult.

No extended argument on this subject was offered, either because the San Pedro people were not yet sufficiently sure of their ground, or else because it was thought the case was strong enough on the technical merits of the two harbors. As we have said before, the so-called "monopoly" feature of the harbor, which was afterwards the subject of so much discussion, was at this time seldom referred to.

That there was a disposition on the part of the San Pedro people to regard the decision of this Board as a finality—whatever it might be—shows very clearly in the utterance of Mr. Shorb, who was the acknowledged representative of that side of the case. He said, in beginning his remarks to the Board: "Whatever your decision may be in reference to this point, gentlemen, in behalf of myself, in behalf of the people of Wilmington and San Pedro, we bow absolute submission to your judgment."

While none of the Santa Monica or Southern Pacific speakers put the idea into definite words that appear in the record, it was freely expressed in conversation, and Judge Carpenter showed it in the sentiment of his concluding speech, in which he said:

But after all, gentlemen of the Board, the question comes down to a matter of engineering, a matter of figures; and that you will determine from the proof that has been and will be laid before you. We want what is fair. We want no aspersions cast upon anybody, without some proof. We have cast none upon the other side. We have abused nobody; we have denounced nobody; we have questioned nobody's motives, and we humbly submit that nobody has a right, in the name of morality or conscience, or any other thing, to question ours, until there is some proof that they are wrong.

We stand upon our manhood and our rights. We can

defend Santa Monica without asperging or lying about or abusing San Pedro or Redondo or any railroad under heaven. We stand upon the bottom of truth and justice and commercial economy, and the best interests of the people of Southern California; and that is a platform that will stand, when all these miserable insinuations, with their authors, are buried in eternal oblivion.

The report of the Board was filed October 27, 1892, and was presented to Congress and referred to the Committee on Rivers and Harbors December 7.

It is an interesting and comprehensive document, and practically completes the case for San Pedro from the technical point of view. It failed to touch on the question of the Southern Pacific control of Santa Monica, either to absolve it from the charge or to condemn it. But the Board did consider, with practical thoroughness, the question of the national commercial necessity for a harbor in Southern California near Los Angeles.

After a brief introduction, describing the work of the Board, the report takes up the general topic of commercial and naval relations, as follows :*

> Santa Monica and San Pedro bays are situated upon the southern coast of California, between Point Dume and Point Lasuen. Santa Monica bay extends from Point Dume to Point Vincente, and San Pedro bay from Point Fermin to Point Lasuen. Back of this portion of the coast lie the counties of Los Angeles, Orange, and San Bernardino, which include the most productive and valuable territory in Southern California. The good lands in this region are situated generally close together and are easily accessible by land or sea. The facilities for irrigation are excellent and capable of great future extension. Owing to these advantages this territory is now, and doubtless will continue to be the most important in the Southern part of the State.
>
> The commercial center of this region is the city of Los Angeles, which is situated about thirteen miles from the

---

* It has been thought advisable to present the report of the Craighill Board almost in full, as it constitutes the best technical treatise on the merits of the two harbors. The report of the Walker Board, which considered the same topic two years later, is more voluminous and represents a greater amount of thorough investigation, but its conclusions are practically identical with those of the Craighill report, and it offers very little material that is really new.

RELIEF MAP OF LOS ANGELES COUNTY.

nearest point on the coast. This city has grown with great rapidity, and has now a population of about 55,000. It is not only the principal city of the most productive district, but it is also the point of intersection of all the southern transcontinental and coastwise railway lines, and it will probably always be the most important city of Southern California.

Owing to the topography of the country the natural ocean outlet of this region must be found between Points Dume and San Juan Capistrano; in other words, either in Santa Monica or San Pedro bay. High mountain ranges, requiring heavy grades, expensive to work, obstruct its communication with the port of San Diego, the only harbor on the south; and on the north the approaches to the coast are difficult, and there is no good harbor nearer than San Francisco bay.

The principal products of this region are oranges and other fruits, wines and brandies, vegetables and grain. By far the larger part of these products is transported by the railways, the most advantageous and extensive markets being found in our own country. The only shipping ports for the part transported by water along the coast or to foreign countries are the harbor of Wilmington, situated at the northwestern end of San Pedro bay, and the wharf at Redondo Beach, near the southern extremity of Santa Monica bay. The Southern Pacific Company is now constructing an extensive wharf a short distance west of Santa Monica canyon.

A general idea of the volume and character of the seaport business transacted at the present time may be formed from the following statistics, which relate to the year 1891. The number of coasting vessels which arrived during the year at Wilmington was 546, and at Redondo 255, and 41 vessels, entered from foreign ports, making a total of 842 vessels. The principal export was wheat, the value of which was about $40,000. The principal imports from foreign countries were coal, cement and glass, the value of which was about $370,000. The value of the coal, most of which comes from Australia, was about $340,000. The imports in coasting vessels at Wilmington were 53,643,060 feet of lumber, 342,525 railway ties, and 14,358 tons of other articles; and at Redondo 20,689,464 feet of lumber, and 29,179 tons of other articles.

It will appear from the above that the maritime exports of this region are at present insignificant, and that the imports from foreign ports, with the exception of coal, are of little consequence. The coastwise traffic, consisting principally of the importation of lumber, forms by far the most important part of the seaport business. The existing harbor facilities for the accommodation of this traffic consist of the port of Wilmington, the improved channel of which has a minimum depth of about 14 feet at mean low water, and at the port of Redondo, at whose wharf, it is stated, vessels of the largest draft can lie with perfect safety, except for a few days in the year. The landing facilities will be considered more fully in a subsequent part of this report. They are now briefly mentioned to show that the present demands of commerce, either for safety or convenience, do not appear to be such as would justify the construction of a deep-water harbor at great expense by the general government.

By far the most important aspect of this subject, however, is its relation to the probable future development of the deep-sea commerce of the country. Heretofore the Asiatic trade has naturally gone to San Francisco, but it has been pointed out that the construction of the Canadian and Northern Pacific railroads has introduced two competitors for the overland transportation of the Asiatic commerce. Two through lines, the Southern Pacific and the Santa Fe systems, cross the continent from Los Angeles at much lower elevations than the northern lines, and also connect the Pacific with the Gulf of Mexico, and their operation is never obstructed by snow or ice. If a safe, accessible and convenient harbor for deep-draft vessels existed on the southern coast these would appear the most favorable lines for the transportation of Asiatic and Australian commerce.

Should the Nicaragua canal be completed the importance of the proposed harbor will become still greater. At the present time the most convenient course for sailing vessels coming around the Horn is to go out into the mid-Pacific and strike the trade winds to make the port of San Francisco. With the completion of the canal, commerce will be principally transported by steam vessels of moderate draft, which will move north along the coast and seek the nearest favorable and convenient port from which their freight can reach its market.

A deep-water harbor on the southern coast would thus receive the Asiatic and Australian freights for shipment over the most favorable transcontinental lines, accommodate a large part of the commerce passing through the Nicaragua canal which now goes around the Horn, and finally furnish a port of shipment and supply not only for the productive territory in its immediate vicinity, but also for the great interior plateau reached by the southern railways beyond the mountain ranges. Considering, therefore, the probable needs of commerce in the near future, the board is of the opinion that the proposed deep-water harbor is of high national importance and well worthy of construction by the general government.

As regards the naval necessities of the country, it must be remarked that the harbor of San Diego is in location, accessibility, anchorage area, and defensive capacity better adapted to the purposes of a naval rendezvous than any artificial deep-water harbor which can be constructed on this part of the coast. This harbor is near the Mexican frontier. The entrance is easily approached, and there are no outlying dangers. The minimum depth over the bar at mean low water is now 21 feet, which is to be increased to 26 feet under the adopted project for improvement, and the deep-water anchorage within covers an area of about 933 acres. As already indicated, this harbor does not fully satisfy the conditions of a great commercial port for the service of the country northwest of it, owing to unfavorable topographical conditions; but these conditions do not affect its supremacy for naval purposes.

Nevertheless, Santa Monica and San Pedro bays furnish convenient landing place from which an enemy could readily conduct hostile operations against Southern California, and it is therefore of the highest importance that the location of a harbor in this vicinity should be selected with special reference to its capacity for easy and efficient defense.

The conclusions of the board, with reference to the relations of the proposed deep-water harbor to the commercial and naval necessities of the country, may be summarized as follows: The present interests of the coastwise and foreign transportation of Southern California do not justify the construction of such a harbor, although they would doubtless be benefited thereby; but the prospective requirements of foreign commerce amply warrant the government in its establishment, even at large expense. The location of such a harbor should be determined principally with reference to the convenient and ample accommodation of deep-draft vessels engaged in foreign trade and the requirements of ships of war, the needs of the coastwise navigation and the cost of construction being considered matters of secondary importance.

Then follows a detailed technical description of the topography of the section and its general meteorological conditions. Then the board says:

It appears, then, that Santa Monica bay is entirely open to the moderate down-coast or west winds which prevail during the greater part of the year, and that it also is exposed to the dangerous winds and seas which occur during the winter months, coming from the south and southwest. The degree of exposure is, however, not absolutely equal in all parts of the bay. The easterly end, near Malaga Cove, is afforded protection from the winds and seas from the south by the high land to the southward, which also affords partial protection from the southwest seas. Catalina island also aids in some degree to shelter this portion of the bay from southerly seas.

On the other hand, Santa Monica bay is entirely sheltered from the southeast winds by the high lands of San Pedro hill.

San Pedro bay is protected by the same high land from the prevailing down-coast wind. In ordinary weather the Bay of San Pedro is quiet and vessels lie safely at anchor, and for the most part discharge cargo with lighters while the wind prevails. It was doubtless this circumstance which made this point the embarcadero of this part of the coast for the Mexican trade before California was acquired by the Americans. In more recent times the greater part of the commerce of this part of the country has also been transacted here. Formerly all the deep-draft vessels from Australia and Puget Sound discharged cargoes in this bay. Recently one of these ships discharged at the wharf at Redondo.

San Pedro bay is also protected to a great extent from the southwest sea and wind by the island of Santa Catalina, which lies about 18 miles off shore to the windward. This island is 17½ miles in length and its height of 1,500 to 2,000 feet makes its shelter, as far as it extends, complete. It covers 48 degrees of the total arc of exposure from southwest seas, but leaves uncovered the angle between the westerly end of the island and Point Fermin, through which interval the direct southwest swells reach the San Pedro anchorage.

San Pedro bay is also directly exposed to the southeast seas, which approach through the interval between Point San Juan and the easterly end of Catalina island. While the winds and seas from the southeast are not regarded as formidable, those from points farther around to the south, that enter through the open space last referred to, are considered to be heavier and more violent than those that approach the anchorage ground from the westward of Catalina.

The record of vessels wrecked at San Pedro shows that, with one exception, the disasters occurred during the southerly storms, the heavy sea coming to the eastward of Catalina island. The vessels were driven ashore on the west line of the bay. Among those lost were the Nicholas Biddle, Callao, Adelaide Cooper, San Luis American, R. P. Buck, and the Kennebec. The exception noted was that of the Amy, which was driven ashore at Point Fermin during a northeast storm from the Santa Ana wind gap.

The arc of exposure at Santa Monica, extending from Point Dume on the west to Point Vincente on the east, is 101 degrees, at Ballona 104 degrees, and at Redondo 90 degrees. Leaving out of consideration the last named point, regarded as impracticable on account of depth, we may call the arc of exposure of Santa Monica Bay 102 degrees. From Point Fermin as a center, the arc of exposure of San Pedro bay around to the west of Catalina island is 60 degrees. The arc protected by the island is 48 degrees, and the arc included between the easterly end of the island and Point Loma is 42 degrees, making the total exposure of San Pedro bay to southeast and southwest winds and seas 102 degrees. The aggregate angle of exposure of the two bays is therefore the same.

A memorandum kindly furnished by Prof. Geo. Davidson, of the U. S. Coast and Geodetic Survey, a disinterested and able observer, to whose opinions the board attaches the highest value, contains the following interesting information with reference to storms and exposure along this part of the coast: In the southeasters the swell of the Pacific comes from the southwest, and along the greater part of the coast of California breaks squarely upon the shore, reaching from profound depths at a very short distance from the land. The only fairly protected part of the coast is that from Point Concepcion eastward and southward to between San Pedro and San Diego. The winter storms of this coast have, however, a marked peculiarity; the gales increase in violence as we proceed to the north. In the low latitude of Santa Monica and San Pedro bays the winter storms are comparatively moderate, and the great islands of Santa Barbara form barriers against the full force of the winter swell. A strong evidence of the weakness of the destructive action of the southeast storms is seen in the very slow wearing away of the sandy cliffs, and of the bluffs at San Pedro; nor could the exposed wharves be maintained in this region if the destructive action of the storms were great.

In order to effect a satisfactory comparison, it became necessary for the board to select the exact location for a breakwater in each of the sites that were considered, and this discussion, which is entirely technical in its character, occupies several pages of the report.

After considering the idea of a floating breakwater the board dismisses Redondo with this paragraph:

The board is of the opinion that it would not be advisable for the government to undertake the costly and doubtful experiment of establishing a floating breakwater at Redondo, especially as such a shelter is not needed for the protection of life or property, but merely for the occasional convenience of navigation.

In concluding its discussion of the subject of breakwater sites, the board says:

For the purpose of comparison, the board adopts the breakwater locations indicated by the Board of Engineers, of 1890, opposite Santa Monica village, and by the chief engineer of the Southern Pacific Company, above Santa Monica canyon, as they are considered as favorable as any sites in these localities.

As before remarked, the project of the board of 1890 for the formation of a harbor at San Pedro proposes the construction of two breakwaters covering an area east of Point Fermin from the southeast and southwest seas. An opening of 1,500 feet is left between them to afford an entrance to the harbor from the westward and to provide for the circulation of the littoral currents.

This plan is shown to be open to serious objections, and the board recommends a different one·

The board recommends a single, curved breakwater, extending southward and eastward from Point Fermin, substantially as shown on the accompanying drawings, subject to such modifications in detail, as experience during the progress of the work may show to be necessary or expedient. Such a breakwater will present no salient angles to the attacks of the sea, no re-entrant angles to compress the moving wave, and it can be extended eastward should t'. necessities of commerce require it. Its length is 8,200 feet, being 200 feet more than the aggregate length of the two breakwaters proposed by the board of 1890. Should further investigation demonstrate the desirability of a western opening, a result which the board does not anticipate, the plan can be modified accordingly.

Then begins the comparison of the various locations:

As a basis for the comparison of the relative advantages of the locations proposed in Santa Monica and San Pedro bays, the board invites attention to the following propositions, which were briefly referred to in the beginning of this report:

The harbor to be formed is not primarily a harbor of refuge, but a port of commerce. It should be located and designed with special reference to the requirements of deep-draft vessels engaged in foreign trade, because this trade promises to be of the greatest national importance in the future, and because such vessels, after long voyages especially, need convenient and commodious places for refitting and supply. The accommodation of the coasting trade is of secondary importance, but it should receive due consideration. From a national point of view the capacity of the harbor for defense is a matter of the highest moment, since an indefensible commercial port is simply an invitation to attack in time of war. We have now too many such ports, and it is not desirable to increase the number. Finally, the relative cost of harbor construction and maintenance should be considered.

The questions, therefore, which require examination are as follows:

First—The comparative advantages of each location as a point of arriving and departure, especially for deep-draft vessels engaged in the foreign trade.

Under this head we must consider the character of the approaches from the sea as regards facility of navigation with the prevailing winds, the safety from hidden danger, and the distance from commercial ports.

Second—The comparative advantages of each location as a place of shelter and for receiving and discharging freight.

Under this head we must consider the extent of anchorage area and its exposure to wind and sea; the extent and shelter of frontage for landing facilities; the capacity of the harbor for extension when required by the future demands of commerce; and the character of the holding ground.

Third—The comparative advantages of each location for land communication with the commercial center.

Under this head we must consider the number of railroad lines, the distance by rail, and the grades and curves on each line.

Fourth—The comparative adaptability of each location for harbor construction and maintenance.

Under this head we must consider the amount of natural shelter afforded by the position; the suitability of the foundation for the breakwater; the comparative facility and cost of construction; the exposure to injuries requiring repair, and the probable permanence of the harbor as regards shoaling.

Fifth—The relative capacity of each location for defense.

On the first point, that of the comparative advantages for arrival and departure, the board holds that there is no essential difference between the locations of San Pedro and Santa Monica.

On the subject of the advantages for shelter and for handling freight, the board says:

For the purposes of comparison, the anchorage areas for the Santa Monica harbors are assumed to be areas included within the breakwaters, the lines drawn through their ends normal to the shore, and the 6-foot contour; and for the San Pedro Harbor the area included between the breakwater, the line drawn from the end of the breakwater to Deadman's Island, and the 6-foot contour. The deep-water anchorage is assumed to be an area over which there is a depth of at least 30 feet; the remaining area will be referred to as the inner anchorage.

The total anchorage area at the San Pedro harbor is 1187 acres. This includes the area in Wilmington Harbor. The deep-water area is 339 acres and the inner anchorage area

846 acres. The harbor at Santa Monica village has a total anchorage of 1078 acres. The deep-water area is 602 acres and the inner anchorage 476 acres. The harbor above Santa Monica canyon has a total anchorage area of 994 acres. The deep-water area is 479 acres and the inner anchorage 515 acres. In the Santa Monica harbors the inner anchorage will be very much diminished by the wharves, which must extend completely across it to reach deep water. This is not the case to the same extent in the San Pedro Harbor.

To compare the exposures, it is assumed that so much of the anchorage area as lies north of southeast and southwest lines drawn through the ends of the breakwaters is not fully covered by the heavy swells. The harbor at San Pedro has a protected area of 852 acres and an unprotected area of 335 acres. The harbor at Santa Monica village has a protected area of 209 acres and an unprotected area of 869 acres. The harbor above Santa Monica canyon has a protected area of 221 acres and an unprotected area of 773 acres.

The harbor above Santa Monica canyon, within the anchorage limits assumed, has a land frontage 8,000 feet in length, available for the construction of wharves. The harbor at Santa Monica village has a similar land frontage 8,000 feet in length. In the harbor first mentioned, however, the land approach to the wharves is narrow, and not capable of extension except at great expense, and there is no available place for the construction of interior basins. The conformation of the ground is such that free access to the landing facilities of the harbor would not be easily attainable by all parties engaged in the business of land transportation.

At Santa Monica village, on the other hand, the approaches from the land are more open, and at La Ballona an interior basin could be readily formed. At San Pedro there is a land frontage of 4,300 feet in the outer harbor without including the inner line of the breakwater. Since the breakwater is connected with the shore, a railway can be constructed along it, and wharves can be readily projected from its inner face. This advantage would be sacrificed if a western entrance were established. This gives for the outer harbor an additional frontage of 8,000 feet and a total frontage of 12,300 feet. The frontage of the inner harbor is about 4 miles long. The total frontage for the whole harbor is therefore 33,420 feet, or about 6 1-3 miles. The approaches are good, as they include both sides of the harbor, and Wilmington harbor forms a magnificent interior basin.

In every harbor a portion of the area must be more or less exposed, owing to the necessity of providing convenient communication with the sea. In a port of commerce it is of great importance that the harbor should be so located and designed that the landing facilities should be established in the most sheltered part. In the Santa Monica harbors this imperative condition is entirely neglected, the landing facilities being necessarily situated entirely within the exposed area. As a consequence of this, the wharves will not be well protected during storms, and small vessels will crowd the quiet spaces of the deep-water anchorage. At San Pedro harbor the landing facilities are situated within the unexposed area, and small vessels will find their best shelter in bad weather within the inner harbor.

The deep water anchorage area is amply sufficient in all the harbors and can in all be readily extended in the future. In the San Pedro harbor the landing facilities can be greatly extended within the inner harbor without any addition to the outer breakwater. This is not the case in the Santa Monica harbors.

In all the harbors the holding ground is good. Some doubts have been expressed with regard to the character of the holding ground at San Pedro, but after diligent inquiry the board is satisfied that it is as good in this location as in the others.

The board is of the opinion that the location at San Pedro is decidedly the best, considered as a place of shelter and for receiving and discharging freight.

The question of the distance from Los Angeles is declared to be unimportant, by reason of the insignificant difference between the two locations.

On the question of construction, the board after discussing it in all its details, holds that:

The amount of stone required for the construction of the breakwater proposed for San Pedro would be much less than for either of the breakwaters proposed for Santa Monica bay, the area of the profile along the axis of the breakwater at San Pedro being 322,000 square feet and at Santa Monica canyon 351,700 square feet.

The latter breakwater has less volume than the one at Santa Monica village.

In concluding the topic, the board says:

> In connection with this question of the relative cost of maintenance, it should be remarked that the harbor at Wilmington has been established for many years and improved at great expense by the government. It will not, in any event, be abandoned. If, then, another harbor is constructed in this vicinity, the government will be compelled to light, defend, improve, and maintain two harbors where one would answer the purpose.
>
> The board is of the opinion that the location at San Pedro is decidedly the best as regards adaptability for construction and maintenance.

The report does not go into details on the subject of defense, but merely declares that "after careful consideration, it is of the opinion that the location at San Pedro is best and cheapest as regards capacity for defense."

It finally sums up the case in these words:

> Having made a careful and critical examination for a proposed deep-water harbor at San Pedro or Santa Monica bays, as required by law, the board is unanimously of opinion that the location selected by the Board of Engineers of 1890, at the present anchorage at the westerly side of San Pedro bay under Point Fermin, is the "more eligible location for such harbor in depth, width, and capacity to accommodate the largest ocean-going vessels and the commercial and naval necessities of the country."

The board's estimate of the cost of constructing the San Pedro breakwater was as follows:

Substructure—1,434,612 cubic yards, at $1.50	$2,151,918
Superstructure—178,530 cubic yards, at $2	357,060
Contingencies, 15 per cent	376,346
Total	$2,885,324

LONG BEACH ON SAN PEDRO BAY.

CHAPTER X.

A Decision That Did Not Decide.

THE report of the Craighill Board was published in Los Angeles just before the beginning of 1893, and for a brief time it stopped all discussion of the subject of the harbor location. The Santa Monica people declared that a mistake had been made and that the government would some day rue it, but the mischief was done and could not be helped;

CHARLES FORMAN.

the Redondo people said that they would abide by the decision, and would join with Los Angeles to present a united front for San Pedro; the Southern Pacific people said nothing.

The Los Angeles Chamber, believing that the time for neutrality was now at an end, on January 17th appointed Gen. Chas. Forman, as special delegate to Washington. He proceeded immediately to the capital, accompanied by Mr. Gibbon. In order to show that the sentiment of the southwestern community was generally in favor of the development of a deep-sea harbor near Los Angeles, in accordance with the plan of the engineers, the delegates were armed with numerous petitions of business men of all sections of Southern California, Arizona and New Mexico, and with resolutions from the Redlands and Riverside town trustees, from the Boards of Trade of Pasadena, Pomona and San Pedro, from the Supervisors of San Bernardino County and from the State Board of Trade. They were followed presently by joint resolutions from the California Legislature, from the Galveston Chamber of Commerce,* and from various commercial organizations in the Southwestern Territories.

There was no regular River and Harbor bill this year, it being the short session, and the Chamber's representatives were assured that there was no hope of an appropriation for San Pedro. Nevertheless they proceeded to make the most of their opportunity to accomplish some missionary work. Senator Felton introduced a bill for a direct appropriation of $250,000, to begin work at San Pedro in accordance with the project outlined by the Craighill Board, but the measure never made its way out of the Senate Committee on Commerce, of which Mr. Frye was the chairman. Gen. Forman and Mr. Gibbon were given a hearing before this committee. In his report to the chamber, filed March 10, 1893, Gen. Forman says relative to this hearing: "As to the question of location, I explained that, to the people of the Southwest generally, it had heretofore been a matter of no consequence where the harbor was built, whether at Santa Monica, Redondo or San Pedro—their desire being that it should be built somewhere, as soon as possible. The general government having now given the matter a thorough investigation, through two separate boards of engineers, who had reported unanimously in favor of San Pedro as the most available point at which to locate the harbor, there was no longer any opportunity for choice left to our people, and

---

* Agitation was in progress at this time to secure an appropriation of about four million dollars to construct a deep-water harbor at Galveston —an improvement which is now well under way.

for that reason we had all combined to urge the claims of the selected port."

Senator John P. Jones of Nevada, whose real and unofficial home is in Santa Monica, was a member of the Senate Committee on Commerce, and he is the owner of a great deal of land along the water front of that city and about Port Los Angeles, the location of the wharf. His vote and influence were always thrown in favor of the Santa Monica harbor site. He asked Senator Frye that the matter of an appropriation for harbor improvement near Los Angeles should not be considered in his absence from Washington, and this, through the operation of "Senatorial courtesy," prevented any action in the winter of 1893. The statement which was offered at the beginning of the session that no appropriations for river and harbor purposes, except those of a most urgent character, were to be made, was scarcely borne out by the record, which shows that over $22,000,000 was appropriated that year, although $40,000,000 of continuing contracts were outstanding. But San Pedro was not seriously considered by the committee.

In concluding his report to the chamber, Gen. Forman inveighs strongly against any reopening of the location issue, which will, he says, have the effect of upsetting the good work done thus far. "Such a thing," he says, "as Congress appropriating money for the construction of works contrary to the advice of its engineers, would be against all precedents and in the highest degree improbable. As the case now stands with the nation's representatives at Washington, it is San Pedro or nothing. Agitation in favor of any other point would merely result in postponing indefinitely any improvement whatever."

These expressions were evidently called forth by the fact that attempts were even then under way to take up anew the question of where the harbor should be situated, in spite of the "once for all" settlement by the Craighill Board. Such was indeed the case. The work on the long wharf at Santa Monica was being pushed with vigor, and it began to dawn on the merchants of Los Angeles that the Southern Pacific was undertaking a great plan there, which would have a decided bearing on the future commerce of the section. Freight coming to Los Angeles from San Francisco saved half a day's time coming by Santa Monica, as against San Pedro, and the new wharf was a convenient and valuable improvement. The members of the Chamber of Commerce were invited from time to time by the Southern Pacific to go down and visit the work, and a free train was provided for that purpose. On such occasions, the representatives of the road and the Santa Monica people and others expressed great regret that the government had decided in favor of San Pedro, a place which would be of no practical use for the commerce of Los Angeles, instead of Port Los Angeles, the natural location.

In February of 1893, at the very time that Gen. Forman was wrestling with the Commerce Committee of the Senate, the annual banquet of the Chamber of Commerce was held at Redondo, at which the topic of the wharf was discussed, and the policy of the Southern Pacific foreshadowed to some extent by one of its officers.

At this banquet Mr. H. E. Huntington, who is the nephew of Mr. C. P. Huntington, and who was at that time the acting president of the road, was asked to respond to the toast, "The Commerce of the Pacific," and it was intimated to him by the committee that they would be glad if he would tell something of the plans of the road with regard to the new wharf. Mr. Huntington was ill and unable to be present, and Mr W. H. Mills, the Vice-President of the company, and one of its directors, was asked to speak on that topic in his place. Mr. Mills is one of the best speakers in California, eloquent, witty and profound, and he possesses to a remarkable degree the faculty of making the dry topic of commerce, on which he is frequently called to speak, one of vivid interest.

After explaining the absence of Mr. Huntington, which was due to illness, Mr. Mills said:

Mr. Huntington instructed me to say to you that whatever plans you may have for the commercial and industrial development of this part of the State, you have the hearty sympathy and shall have the co-operation of the Southern Pacific Company. However, regarding this wharf and other improvements to which reference has been made, I must tell you that I am not authorized by Mr. Huntington to disclose any of the secrets of the company.

As an industrial student of this State, I have always observed that the shortest line of connection between tide water on the Atlantic and tide water on the Pacific was at some point near Los Angeles. We know, now that railway communication has been established, that the nearest line is between Los Angeles and Galveston. But commerce will not go to Galveston, because it is a law of railroad transportation that every thing must reach its terminal. When a car is loaded and sent on its journey, it must go to its terminal point for its return freight; and therefore, New Orleans, at the mouth of the Mississippi river, the Queen City of the South, will be the Atlantic seaport, which will have for its western terminus Santa Monica.

I wish to say that I had no desire to broach this subject at this time, and I do not speak of it to raise any local question as between San Pedro, Santa Monica and Redondo or any other of the local seaports. There will come a time when all these questions will be forgotten. California is a new country, and we have more or less contention in the early stages of our development. But somewhere on your borders there is to be a harbor, and as I am asked a question regarding Santa Monica, and the intentions of our people, to be frank with you I will say that their intentions seem to me to be entirely apparent. They are making a wharf there for deep-water vessels. They must intend to land at the wharf with deep-water vessels.

These pointed allusions to Santa Monica, as the natural harbor for trans-Pacific commerce, did not pass unnoticed, and it was only a short time after this that the Los Angeles Times, a Republican morning paper of general circulation throughout Southern California, raised the question editorially whether the Southern Pacific people proposed to abide by the decision of the engineering authorities, whom they had invoked, of their own desire, to render a final judgment. The Times had never been regarded as an anti-corporation or anti-Southern Pacific newspaper. Its editor and chief proprietor, Colonel Harrison Gray Otis,* is decidedly conservative in his point of view, and whatever else may be said of him, he certainly possesses

---

* His present title is Brigadier General Otis, which was bestowed on him during the late Spanish war. During the period of this history, however, he was "Colonel" Otis and he will be so styled.

none of the "sand lot," radical element in his make-up. His efforts to place the employees of his establishment on a non-union basis had involved him in a serious conflict with labor organizations, which was raging with great fierceness at this particular time; and the agitators and walking delegates, who were, to a considerable extent, the active spirits of the anti-railway propaganda, were proclaiming against Col. Otis and his paper all over the State. There was reason enough why he should prefer an alliance with the railroad

BRIG. GEN. H. G. OTIS.

rather than opposition to it, had that been possible. The fact that he was one of the first to see into and through the railroad plan, and that he threw the influence of the Times with all the force at its command into the anti-railroad side of the fight, is evidence at once of his discernment and his sincerity.

The opening gun of the Times' battery was an editorial appearing in the spring of 1893, which was the handiwork of W. A. Spalding, the present managing editor of the Los Angeles Herald, at that time an editorial writer on and a stockholder in the Times. In this article the lines of policy for the paper were very clearly drawn, and they were consistently adhered to through the five years of conflict that followed, in all the curves and sinuosities and twistings and changes of front that such a fight could present. The recent Board of Engineers, said the article, in substance, have settled upon San Pedro as the location for the harbor, confirming the judgment of the former board. We have thus a unanimous decision from eight distinguished authorities, based on technical grounds, in favor of that site. It is the invariable custom of Congress to grant appropriations in ac-

W. A. SPALDING.

cordance with the findings of its own engineers. It is therefore idle to discuss the question of the possibility of securing help for another site than San Pedro. The Southern Pacific people are disposed to favor Port Los Angeles, where they are constructing a wharf. Their enterprise in developing commerce through a new port is commendable and will elicit such patronage as it merits; but that is not the real point at issue. The influence of the Southern Pacific at Washington may be great — perhaps greater than it should be — but it cannot reach to the extent of upsetting all the established precedents that govern harbor appropriations, and even if it were so powerful, it would still be the plain duty of the people of this section and their representatives to oppose a scheme to use government funds against the advice of its technical authorities, for the special use and benefit of a single corporation.

It would perhaps scarcely do justice to the Times and its influence in the harbor contest merely to say that the victory for the people's choice could not have been won without it, for the same may be said of several other agencies and individuals, and the fight was full of critical turnings, where if some one had neglected to do just the right thing at the right time, failure must have resulted. No newspaper can be said to control public opinion, but a journal whose circulation permeates every class of society, which is edited with honest purpose and good ability, and which persistently maintains a policy in favor of an object which the best impulses of men feel to be right—even if it is for the moment unpopular—can exercise an influence so powerful as to be almost dominating. These various qualifications the Times possessed. While it is not free from faults, and is, indeed, greatly criticized—as every powerful newspaper must be—for certain characteristics that it possesses, no one will deny that it is a first-class purveyor of news and that it is managed with ability and—taking a long range view of it—with good judgment. Being human, it has made mistakes, without doubt, but its record in that respect is unusually clear. While its circulation is small compared with that of the great newspapers of the great cities, it is large compared with the circulations that prevail on the Pacific coast, and extraordinary when the population of its tributary district is reckoned. In one respect it is to be classed with papers like the Louisville Courier-Journal, the old New York Tribune and Sun, the Chicago Tribune, the St. Louis Globe-Democrat and the Cincinnati Commercial, it is an organ of direct individual, personal influence. The Times is Harrison Gray Otis, and conversely it may be stated—and it forms a handsome object lesson of success—that for a long period of years Harrison Gray Otis was the Times and nothing but the Times.

But if the power and influence of this newspaper was absolutely necessary to the winning of the people's victory in the harbor controversy, it is only fair to say that the controversy itself formed one of the chief corner-stones of the Times' great financial and journalistic success. Before the fight began, the circulation of the Times was but little, if any, more than that of any one of the three other competitors with which it shared the daily field in Los Angeles. During the critical phases of the contest, subscribers flocked to it by the score and the hundred. At the close of the era with which this book has to deal, its circulation was more than that of all its competitors gathered together. And its clientele is not of the ephemeral order that may be hastily rolled up by the cheap sensationalism of the moment, but it is a patronage that is based for the most part on respect for its abilities and confidence in its sincerity. The Times subscriber, while he may speak with regret of certain faults that he finds in it, will, if he is a resident of Los Angeles of ten years' standing, always close with the remark, "But it made a magnificent fight for the harbor."

It is always an open question how much credit a newspaper deserves for the espousal of a popular cause, as against one to which the people are unfriendly; and if that were all there was to the Times' support of San Pedro, it might be dismissed with a word. But it must be remembered that the Times alone, of all the newspapers of Los Angeles, saw fit to take that side of the controversy; and there were powerful business influences, of the order by which newspapers are commonly swayed, that pulled in the opposite direction. Nor was it evident at the outset which was to be the popular side; and there occurred various crises in the midst of the contest when the pendulum of popular favor swung far to the other pole, and the very foundation seemed about to drop out from under the Free Harbor cause. For its courage and its firmness and consistency at such moments, the Times is entitled to credit and admiration; and for this it will receive praise. even from those who fail to approve its course in other respects.

The election of the fall of 1892 had an important bearing on the harbor issue. The effect of the general landslide in the direction of Democracy was felt even as far west as California, which gave its electoral vote to Mr. Cleveland, and sent several Democratic or Fusion Congressmen to Washington from the State, and elected a Democratic Legislature. In the Sixth Congressional district, which at that time included all the Southern and Central section of the State, Hervey Lindley, a Republican of Los Angeles, was defeated by Marion Cannon, a Populist of Ventura, the latter receiving the Democratic vote and also the votes of many Republicans who considered that Mr. Lindley was on altogether too friendly terms with the railroad and its machine.

The Democratic Legislature met in January of 1893 and elected Stephen M. White of Los Angeles to the Senate, the man who was to win the San Pedro appropriation after one of the most extraordinary battles ever fought in the halls of Congress.

CHAPTER XI.

The Chamber of Commerce Takes a Vote.

THE time was now at hand in Los Angeles when the lines were to be drawn between those who favored the railroad choice for a harbor site and those who proposed to abide by the decisions of the engineer boards. The issue was becoming a live one, that could not be evaded. Everybody deplored the existence of the controversy, but each side laid the blame for it upon the other. The Santa Monica partisans denounced their opponents for "fighting the railroad" and alienating thereby a powerful friend, that could either get us the appropriation or keep it eternally out of our reach. On the other hand, the San Pedro element sneered at the "railway crowd," as they were disposed unjustly to call those on the other side, and reiterated the question: how was it proposed to get an appropriation for a spot that had been unanimously damned by two different boards of engineers.

The contest was at first good-natured enough, but, as was inevitable where such considerable interests were at stake, rancor soon crept in. With the Herald and Express supporting the Santa Monica site, against the Times, which favored San Pedro, the hurling of epithets was not long to be deferred. There were cautious and conservative men on both sides, who constantly expressed the fear that the division might terminate in putting off all appropriations for an indefinite period; but the majority of these presently found themselves drawn into the whirl of the combat, and decided that the only way to secure peace was to fight for it. There were also not a few cheerful souls who managed to hold seats in both factions, and some who professed to be strictly "on the fence." But the great majority of the people of Los Angeles found permanent location on one side or the other, and this was especially true of those who held political positions and those who were prominent in public work.

By the beginning of 1894, the long wharf at Santa Monica was about completed, and was thrown open for public use. The enterprise of the railroad was widely commended, and the people of Los Angeles, especially the merchants who would have occasion to ship over the wharf, expressed great gratification at the substantial and useful improvement. A considerable tide of business that had formerly flowed into Los Angeles by way of San Pedro, and later by way of Redondo, was now suddenly transferred to the more northerly port.

Mr. C. P. Huntington was much pleased with the favorable outlook for his new venture, and when the work was completed, he paid it a visit of inspection. While in Los Angeles, he called at the rooms of the Chamber of Commerce, and asked for a conference with some of its officers on the subject of local harbor improvements. The President, Mr. D. Freeman, and Gen. Chas. Forman, one of the vice-presidents, were summoned by telephone, and there were present besides those gentlemen and Mr. Huntington, the Secretary of the Chamber, and the Southern Pacific local agent, Mr. Crawley. The conversation lasted about an hour. Mr. Huntington did a large part of the talking, for the representatives of the Chamber, knowing that the Southern Pacific president was absolutely determined upon a Santa Monica policy, and that the interests of his corporation were considerably involved, forebore to discuss the issue beyond what was required for politeness' sake.

"You people are making a big mistake in supporting this

San Pedro appropriation," said he. "The River and Harbor Committee of the House will never report in favor of that place—not in a thousand years. I know them all, and have talked with them about this matter. The same is true of the Senate Committee on Commerce. The chairman of that committee, Senator Frye, has visited both harbors and he says he will never consent to the expenditure of one dollar for an outside harbor at San Pedro. He thinks it cannot be built, and his mind will not change, no matter how many reports you may get to the contrary. And you know the chairman of that committee is all-powerful in the matter of appropriations."

"But will Congress appropriate money for an improvement against the advice of its engineers?" was asked.

"It has done so on numberless occasions,"* answered Mr. Huntington. "Besides, the engineers have not reported against Santa Monica. They have simply declared that the San Pedro work is somewhat cheaper than the other, and the difference is so small that I would sooner pay it out of my own pocket than have such a mistake made in location as would occur if the harbor were to be built at San Pedro.† Congress is all-powerful in the matter of appropriations, and can do as it sees fit. It can appoint a board with instructions to find in favor of Santa Monica, if it chooses to do so."

"Now, I propose to be frank with you people," continued the Southern Pacific president. "I do not find it to my advantage to have this harbor built at San Pedro, and I shall be

---

* This statement, which was frequently made by the Santa Monica adherents, had but slight basis in fact. It is true that the Government engineers had advised against the experiment of the Eads jetties, and that Congress went ahead in spite of that advice; but the case is scarcely parallel with that of the harbor controversy. The position taken by the engineers in the matter of the Eads jetties was that the experiment would probably not succeed; but the States along the lower Mississippi demanded, in their desperation that something be done, and the jetties were finally constructed, according to the plans of private engineers. No other examples of any importance were ever quoted.

† If the reader will examine the report of the Craigill Board, Chapter IX, he will find that cost is only one of a number of counts in the indictment against Santa Monica.

compelled to oppose all efforts that you or others make to secure appropriations for that site; on the other hand, the Santa Monica location will suit me perfectly, and if you folks will get in and work for that, you will find me on your side—and I think I have some little influence at Washington—as much as some other people, perhaps."

Mr. Huntington then proceeded to tell of his plans with reference to trans-Pacific commerce over the Santa Monica wharf, covering much the same line as the banquet speech of W. H. Mills a year before. The Chamber's representatives were much interested, and asked a number of questions on this topic; but on the harbor issue they were dumb, and even Mr. Huntington's direct inquiries failed to bring satisfactory answers.

At the very conclusion of the interview, Mr. Huntington showed for the first time his decided animus in the matter. He brought down his fist with some force on the desk where he sat, and said: "Well, I don't know, for sure, that I can get this money for Santa Monica; I think I can. But I know damned well that you shall never get a cent for that other place."

He rose to his feet, his face a little flushed with annoyance or anger, but a moment later was smiling pleasantly, as he proposed that the Chamber's Board of Directors go down to Santa Monica the next day in his private car, and inspect the wharf.

The invitation was accepted, and about a dozen members of the Board went in the party the following day. They visited the wharf, and then repaired to the Arcadia Hotel, where some wine was served, and where Mr. Huntington proved a most agreeable host.

No publication was made of this conference at the time, and very little was ever said about it, as those who were present, representing the chamber, were anxious to avoid rousing any ill-will on the harbor subject, and it was feared that Mr. Huntington's threat, if it became generally known, might increase the growing bitterness.

In the month of September, 1892, about the time of the meeting of the Craighill Board, Mr. J. M. Crawley, the Southern Pacific local representative, prepared a petition asking that the deep-sea harbor appropriation, if one should be allotted to this section, should go to Santa Monica, instead of San Pedro, and he secured to this document the signatures of eighty-three of the leading merchants of Los Angeles, particularly those engaged in wholesale trade and importing, and the signatures represented business capital amounting to over ten million dollars.

The names were carefully selected and the list very nearly covered the field. Mr Crawley afterwards declared that only a few who were approached refused to sign it, and that all the others signed cheerfully and without discussion. This list was frequently referred to thereafter by the railroad to demonstrate that, whatever the popular sentiment might be on the subject of the harbor, the mercantile influence was in favor of Santa Monica. Against this it was urged that many of the merchants felt themselves compelled to sign the petition to continue friendly relations with the road, and that others signed it under a misapprehension, supposing that it was merely a request to the government to "do something for Santa Monica." But whatever value the petition may have had as showing the status of public opinion prior to the decision of the Craighill Board, it was certainly inoperative after that decision had been rendered.

On the 7th day of March, 1894, eighteen months after the names had been gathered, Mr. Crawley appeared before the Directors of the Chamber of Commerce, and presented this petition, and asked that action be taken in accordance with it.

"The gentlemen who sign this document," said Mr. Crawley addressing the board, "are all active members of your organization, and their names are fairly representative of the mercantile element of the community. I am informed that your organization is about to adopt some resolutions on the question of the harbor site, and is considering the advisability of sending a special delegate to Washington to represent the commercial interests of this section. Now I ask, as a member of this organization, and as representing a corporation which is largely interested in the welfare of Southern California, that you act as this petition suggests, and resolve in favor of appropriations for Santa Monica.

Consideration of Mr. Crawley's request was deferred until the next meeting of the board, which took place March

14th, and at this a lively discussion began, which was protracted by one parliamentary device or another from meeting to meeting for nearly a month. At the outset, there seemed to be no reason to doubt that the board would be for San Pedro by a good working majority. Less than a year previous, this same body had, by a unanimous vote, passed a resolution strongly in favor of the site selected by the engineers, and had sent Gen. Forman to Washington to present that side of the case. To follow Mr. Crawley's suggestion involved a complete and rather humiliating change of front. Kaspare Cohn, a large shipper of wool, and a man of high standing in the community, offered the resolutions in favor of Santa Monica. They read as follows:

> Whereas, By reason of the close proximity of Santa Monica to Los Angeles, and the rapid and continuous growth of the city of Los Angeles toward Santa Monica, unmistakable evidence to all that in time the western boundary of the city of Los Angeles will be the ocean front at Santa Monica; and
>
> Whereas, The greater distance and the topography of the country between Los Angeles and San Pedro are barriers to the growth of the City of Los Angeles in the direction of San Pedro; and
>
> Whereas, There is now built at Santa Monica a wharf 4660 feet in length, reaching to a point where there is 40 feet of water at high tide, thus bringing ships of the deepest draft and cars together; and
>
> Whereas, It is desirable that the freight intended for Los Angeles and this section of the State, which is loaded in vessels at ports on the Atlantic Coast, at Panama, and ports in Mexico, and which now passes Santa Monica and is taken to San Francisco and again shipped to Los Angeles, and this part of the State, thereby increasing the cost of such freight, that it should be unloaded from vessels at the nearest point to Los Angeles; and
>
> Whereas, Eighty-three of the merchants of Los Angeles, representing about ten million dollars of capital, fully realizing the situation, and viewing it from a commercial standpoint, have subscribed to a petition, copy of which accompanies this resolution, urging that Santa Monica be selected as the proper place where a breakwater should be constructed; now, therefore, be it

Resolved: That the Chamber of Commerce, representing as it does, the commercial interests of the city of Los Angeles, do make known to our Senators and Representatives at Washington that for the reasons set forth above we believe the construction of a breakwater and the creation of a harbor at Santa Monica will best serve our commercial interests, and that such action will receive the strong support of the people; and we do hereby pray Congress that an appropriation be made for that purpose, independent of any appropriation which may be needed to maintain in good condition what is known as the inner harbor of San Pedro and Wilmington.

Mr. L. N. Breed, a banker, offered a compromise resolution in line with the plan which two years later came to be known as the "double appropriation scheme." It asked that money be appropriated to construct a deep-water harbor at Santa Monica, and also to dredge out and improve the inner harbor at San Pedro.

Mr. W. C. Patterson, a wholesale produce merchant, who afterwards became president of the Chamber, and who was to the end a most effective worker in the Free Harbor cause, proposed the following:

Whereas, the Board of Directors of the Chamber of Commerce is in receipt of a petition from Mr. J. M. Crawley of the Southern Pacific Company, asking that we call upon our representatives at Washington to favor an appropriation for Santa Monica instead of San Pedro, and

Whereas, Three separate commissions of United States Engineers, appointed to examine the coast and decide upon a proper location for a deep-water harbor in this vicinity have unanimously declared in favor of San Pedro, and

Whereas, It is the invariable custom of Congress in cases of this character to refuse all appropriations that are not in accordance with the decisions of its engineers; therefore be it

Resolved, That in the opinion of this Board of Directors an appeal to our representatives to support an appropriation for Santa Monica would, under the most favorable circumstances, result only in the appointment of a fourth commission who would probably make the same report as their predecessors.

Resolved, That we see at the present time no cause to attempt to reverse the action invariably taken by this board and by the members of the chamber when called together to consider this question, and that we now again place ourselves on record as favoring an appropriation to begin the work on the outer harbor at San Pedro.

Resolved, That we call upon the people and press and public organizations of Los Angeles and Southern California to stand firmly together on this proposition, and not allow themselves to be confused or divided by the claim that the influence of any individual or corporation can prevail against the repeated and emphatic reports of the government engineers, and that we warn our people that agitation in favor of any other place than the one recommended by the engineers is destined to result only in delaying still further the construction of the needed harbor.

The sessions of the board were supposed to be executive, but a reporter of the Express managed to smuggle himself into the room as an assistant clerk, and remained there through the whole of the session. The next day the members of the Chamber became aware, through the publication of the debate, that the board was anything but unanimous on the subject of the harbor site, and the discussion was taken up in earnest all over the city. Henry T. Hazard, who was at that time Mayor of the city, led the debate in the board on the San Pedro side, seconded by Mr. Patterson and Gen. Forman; and the principal Santa Monica advocates were Mr. James B. Lankershim and Mr. Breed.

On three different occasions when the matter was about to come to a vote, an adjournment was secured. In the course of the long debate, Santa Monica gained and San Pedro lost. At first it was the Santa Monica men that dared not come to a vote, but in the end the conditions were reversed, and it was clear that if a decision was reached in the board, it must be against the site selected by the engineers.

Had the vote been won for Santa Monica, it would have supplied the partisans of that side with what was their most serious lack through the whole of the contest, viz., an authoritative public expression in favor of their site. It might also have served permanently to divide public sentiment, which would have made the victory that much the more difficult of winning. The Chamber of Commerce, having thus reversed its position, would have lost its standing with the people of Los Angeles, and if it had not actually gone to pieces under the strain, it would at least have been seriously crippled, and incapacitated from giving the help in the contest that was afterwards so much needed. In short, this was a critical moment in the battle, and all who were concerned felt it to be so at the time.

There was a provision in the constitution of the Chamber, which had never before been put into use, whereby, if the

W. C. PATTERSON.

members were dissatisfied with the action of the board in any matter, a petition to the president, signed by the requisite number of names, would compel the calling of a general meeting, at which all could vote. When it became evident that, if the board took action — and it could not well be longer postponed—the result would be a change of front for the Chamber, Gen. Edward Bouton started a petition addressed to President Freeman, asking that a vote be taken by ballot among the members of the Chamber, as to whether that organization was to advocate one site or the other.

The membership of the chamber at that time was about 550. The date fixed by the president for the ballot was less than a week away, and during that short period a very lively campaign was waged. The Times published each day a series of strong editorial leaders, some of which were written

H. Z. OSBORNE.

by Col. Otis himself, and others by Mr. Spalding, but the greater number by Harry Ellington Brook, who for the past twelve years has been an editorial writer on the Times, and whose devotion to the San Pedro cause had much to do with the efficiency of that paper's service. The Express, under the management of Col. H. Z. Osborne, and the Herald, under the management of Messrs. J. J. Ayers and J. D. Lynch, espoused the Santa Monica cause with considerable force and skill.

The Terminal Railway took an active hand in the fight, and issued a printed pamphlet which contained the full report of the Craighill Board in favor of San Pedro. The Santa Fe, which had up to this time stood aloof, was now drawn into the conflict, and from this time on its influence was thrown in favor of the San Pedro cause. Every mail brought showers of circulars and letters to the members of the Chamber; there were excursions to Santa Monica and San Pedro, and doubtful voters were kept busy dodging the campaign committees of one side or the other.

The ballot was held April 7, 1894, and lasted from nine in the morning until five in the afternoon. It was conducted on the Australian system; each voter went to a table by himself and stamped his ballot with a rubber stamp "For San Pedro" or "For Santa Monica." Members of the board served as tellers, equally divided between the two factions. A considerable amount of feeling was shown to exist by the utterances of many who came to vote, although the principals to the affair, particularly the railway men, remained good-natured.

When the ballots were counted, it was found that 464 had been cast, of which 5 were scattering and the others were divided as follows:

San Pedro 328
Santa Monica 131

Public sentiment of Los Angeles, as evidenced by the vote of its recognized commercial representative, was for the ancient port by a majority of more than two to one.

CHAPTER XII.

THE WINTER OF OUR DISCONTENT.

THE vote in the Chamber of Commerce was regarded as another "final settlement" of the harbor issue, as far as a division among the people of Los Angeles was concerned. A number of citizens who had supported the Santa Monica site, finding by this fair test of public sentiment that the great majority of the active men of the city preferred San Pedro, decided to go in with the majority, and thereafter became enthusiastic workers on the side against the railroad.

"It is evident," said they, "if we are to win any harbor appropriation, that all must pull together for one place.

A vote has been taken, and the majority is for San Pedro. In the face of that vote, we cannot ask the others to come to our way of thinking; we must, therefore, go over to theirs."

By a unanimous vote the Directors of the Chamber now passed the Patterson resolutions, supplemented with a statement of the ballot of the members of the organization. It was decided to send as a special delegate to Washington Col. S. O. Houghton, who had secured the first appropriation for

GEORGE S. PATTON.

San Pedro twenty-five years before. When the time came for his departure, Col. Houghton found himself unable to go, and Geo. S. Patton, a bright young man of Southern origin, eloquent as a speaker and well-informed on the harbor topic, was chosen in his place.

This was, it will be remembered, the long session of the first congress of the Cleveland administration, the session when the fight over the Wilson tariff bill was carried clear through the summer. Both House and Senate were Democratic, and Mr. Frye was compelled to give up the chairmanship of the Committee on Commerce to Ransom of North Carolina.

Mr. Gibbon was present at the beginning of the session, early in 1894, but had been recalled to Los Angeles when the division occurred in the Chamber of Commerce. After the vote was taken, with a favorable result which his efforts had in no small degree assisted to bring about, he returned to Washington, accompanied by Mr. Patton.

Owing to the presence of Mr. White on the Senate Committee on Commerce, it was decided to make the effort to get a San Pedro item into the River and Harbor bill by amendment in the Senate. It was a most unusual thing for a new Senator, one who had not even seen service in the lower house, to receive a place on that important committee, but Mr. White's eminence in the party, and the great reputation for ability and industry which he had brought with him from California, made his appointment to that position possible.

Mr. White is a fearless and a determined character, and, when he believes in any cause, is open and aggressive in fighting its battles. Now that the six years of his service in Congress are at an end, and may be regarded in their entirety, one may pause in wonder and admiration over the unique career that they represent. It is not merely that Mr. White is an orator of exceptional power and force, nor that he is a lawyer of profound reasoning power and broad range of judgment, nor that he understands men and can influence and control their actions—all these things might be true of him, and yet he would not be the man we know now as Stephen M. White. It is his sincerity and his courage that would remain as the distinguishing marks of his public career, even if all else were to be forgotten. At a time when the people of this country were resolved, by a majority so great as to be literally overwhelming, that war should be declared against Spain, when even the warning note from the President that the nation was not prepared for the contest failed to hold the tide in check, and when the only ground for discussion in Congress was not whether nor why we should declare war, but merely how and when, there was one man, and we may almost say only one, who rose to urge with all the force of logic and eloquence at his command, that the country pause before it should undertake a war which he regarded as at once causeless and full of danger. It is not a question now of whether he was right or wrong in his judgment and his premonitions; he had not the favor of the galleries, for the report says they listened in absolute silence though with the closest attention; he had

SENATOR STEPHEN M. WHITE.

not the support of his fellow Senators, for on every amendment and on the main issue the vote went heavily against him; but it was the calmness and deliberation of the speech, its broad, statesman-like view and the splendid courage and honesty of the speaker, that challenged admiration then, as they do now.

The people of Los Angeles are perhaps too near to Mr. White to be able to form a correct judgment of his character. Many of them have oscillated between an unbounded admiration at one time and a disposition to criticise at another. When he entered the Senate, great things were expected of him—things which were finally realized, for at the end of his term he had achieved a position in the very first rank of American Senators—but at first there was a disappointment. Mr. White was expected to throw himself with vigor into the harbor controversy, and to use plain language where it would be heard by the whole nation. But through the first two years, he did his duty by the harbor issue—and he seemed to do no more. When special delegates came on to Washington from Los Angeles, he presented them to the Commerce Committee and arranged for their hearing. He spoke for San Pedro himself with clearness and skill on each available opportunity before the committee, and on two occasions before the Senate. But there was lacking the fire and determination and persistency that had been expected. We know now that he was pursuing the wisest course; that he was saving his influence, guarding and strengthening it, for the time when it would prove most effective in actual result; and that he understood, as no one else did, the tremendous power wielded by the Huntington lobby in Washington.

In the month of June the Commerce Committee of the Senate gave a hearing to the San Pedro-Santa Monica question. The Los Angeles representatives stated their case and were followed by Mr. C. P. Huntington, who appeared in person, and asked that an appropriation of $4,000,000 be made for the breakwater at Port Los Angeles. Mr. Hood repeated his objections to San Pedro, and after him came E. L. Corthell, a riparian engineer of national eminence, who stated that he had looked over the two harbors at the request of Mr. Huntington, and had found Santa Monica much the superior. He asserted among other things that the currents along the shore at San Pedro were from east to west, and that sand would be carried into the harbor in large quantities, necessitating constant dredging. This statement, which was reiterated thereafter by all who supported the Santa Monica side, was denied at the time by Mr. Gibbon, who narrated the fact, known to all residents on San Pedro bay, that lumber or coal washed overboard at San Pedro, always drifts easterly, and comes ashore in the neighborhood of Long Beach. Two years later, the Walker

Board gave a thorough consideration to the matter of currents, and Mr. Corthell's theory was finally ruled out.*

The contest in the committee was prolonged through several weeks, and it was not until the middle of July that a decision was reached. In the beginning the San Pedro advocates thought they had to face merely the issue of an appropriation for that place or no appropriation at all; but they presently discovered that the Santa Monica location, which had received no commendation from the engineers, and for which no one except Mr. Huntington put in a claim, could count a number of determined friends on the committee, and it was apparently to be a question of Santa Monica or nothing. This situation had been fairly outlined by Senator White some months previous in a telegram to Mr. D. Freeman, the president of the Chamber, who at the time the election was about to take place, had applied to Mr. White for his opinion as to San Pedro's chances; and the latter had responded, with perhaps more of truth and sincerity than discretion, that the feeling in the Senate Committee was in favor of Santa Monica rather than San Pedro, and that any effort to get an appropriation for the latter point would involve a hard fight with uncertain issue. Mr. Freeman handed the telegram to a careless person, who allowed it to fall into a grate fire that was burning in the room—and it was promptly forgotten. Had it been made public just at that time, the vote in the Chamber of Commerce might have gone the other way, with what consequences it is hard to tell. The what-might-have-beens of history are sometimes very interesting. Mr White's purpose in sending the telegram—if he had a purpose beyond that of giving truthfully the information for which he was asked—was this: he knew that Mr. Freeman, and the moving spirits in the Chamber of Commerce, were not likely to be turned aside from their purpose to secure a competitive harbor for Los Angeles, by the mere knowledge that the path was beset with difficulty; but, on the other hand they must, by learn-

---

*While the Walker Board was carrying on its investigation in San Pedro Bay, a sailor on the government boat, the Gedney, fell overboard and was drowned near San Pedro. His body was recovered some distance down the shore toward Long Beach—a striking evidence of the error of Mr. Corthell's theory.

ing the truth of the situation, share part of the responsibility for the contest that was about to be undertaken.

Now, for the first time, the attention of the newspapers of the Eastern States began to be attracted to the harbor matter. A combat between the advocates of rival sites for harbor improvement would naturally have but little interest for people removed from the immediate locality that was concerned; but here was an issue that involved questions of grave national importance: Should a harbor be located in accordance with the judgment of the government engineers, based on thorough acquaintance with all the conditions, and in accordance with the wishes of the people of the section, and the demands of all their representatives; or upon the mere *ipse dixit* of one rich and powerful man, whose commercial interest required it in another place? Is this—as the New York World pertinently asked regarding the matter—"Is this a government by the people, for the people, or a government by Mr. Huntington, for Mr. Huntington? The question may as well be settled in the Santa Monica-San Pedro controversy, as anywhere: now, as at any time."

Several New York, Chicago and St. Louis papers published articles on the subject, and the New York World was particularly severe upon Senator Jones, who in those days took an aggressive stand in favor of Santa Monica. Subsequently he grew more moderate, although his vote was always for the Huntington site. This is the way the World puts it (June 26):

> The advantages which the building of an artificial harbor at Santa Monica would bring to Senator Jones personally, it is difficult to overestimate. The official record sheds some light upon the subject. The county records of Los Angeles show that the property adjoining the exclusive water-front of the Southern Pacific is divided into eight holdings. The title to parcels one, two and eight are in the names of John P. Jones and Arcadia B. de Baker. They constitute three-quarters of all the lands situated as described. All the remainder of the land with the exception of a few feet at the mouth of the Santa Monica canyon is in the name of Frank H. Davis, representing Mr. Huntington. It will be seen that Mr. Huntington's Santa Monica enter-

prise throughout its entire extent is as exclusive as though it were surrounded by a Chinese wall.

The St. Louis Globe Democrat contained full reports of the proceedings in committee and from these (June 26 to July 9, 1894) the following paragraphs are culled:

The harbor contest at Los Angeles waxes warmer. C. P. Huntington was seen going the rounds of the hotels to-day, and although it was Sunday, he made no halt in buttonholing Senators. Four days ago there was a decided majority in the Commerce Committee in favor of following the wishes of the two Senators from California, but since the arrival of Mr. Huntington at the capital it is now a matter of great doubt where the majority will be found. There is serious speculation in the minds of many people as to the means Mr. Huntington may have used to bring about this change. . . . . .

For three hours the battle of San Pedro against Santa Monica for government recognition as the Los Angeles harbor waged to-day in the room of the Senate Committee on Commerce. Huntington, the Southern Pacific magnate, paced the corridors, and asked anxiously after news, whenever any one came out of the committee room, and betrayed a degree of nervousness wholly unusual to him. Ordinarily Mr. Huntington is philosophical and composed. To-day he was "rattled" as no one remembers to have seen him, in his many visits to the capital.

One of a series of telegrams, from J. W. Reinhart, president of the Santa Fe, to Mr. R. C. Kerens, shows how much is at stake in this contest: "Atchison is too much interested with its $500,000,000 of property, to permit it to be held out of Pacific ocean business by the Southern Pacific, whose prayer, if granted, would shut out Atchison and create absolute monopoly. Atchison is the only railway line, other than the Southern Pacific, reaching Southern California. If the appropriation goes to Huntington, it throttles all chances of competition, besides permanently injuring the growth of California and adjacent States and Territories."

Mr. Huntington's chief supporters in the committee were Frye of Maine, Jones of Nevada, Dolph of Oregon and the Chairman, Ransom of North Carolina, who had unexpectedly changed from being a San Pedro advocate to a warm admirer of Santa Monica. Although the issue did not come to a straight-out vote, these gentlemen all showed by their expressions in the debate that they were entirely prepared to give Mr. Huntington the $4,000,000 for which he asked. Cullom of Illinois, Berry of Arkansas and White of California were for San Pedro without reservation of any sort. Gorman of Maryland was a San Pedro man, who later switched to the other side. The other members of the committee were either absent or wavering. The result was a drawn battle.

A motion was passed deferring the decision until the next year, "in order," so the resolution read, "to give the members of the Committee on Commerce an opportunity to visit the two harbors and form an opinion on their respective merits." No provision was made for the expenses of the members of the Committee who were to make the trip, and no definite time was set for them to go. It was to be "quite informal." Mr. Frye, who made the motion, announced that he, for one, did not propose to go. Why should he? Had he not looked at both harbors some years ago, and determined then and there that Santa Monica was the better?

This was the so-called "Senatorial Commission," which was to effect another "final settlement," and which never came. The fight over the Wilson bill kept Congress in session all through the summer. In the brief autumnal recess Mr. Cullom visited Los Angeles, inspected the harbors, attended a reception given him by the Illinois people, talked discreetly on the subject of the contest, and then departed. As a device for gaining a year's time "to tire out the people" the Senatorial Commission was decidedly clever; otherwise it did not amount to much. Grave doubt was expressed by the irreverent whether the casual observation of the surface of the waves in a harbor by a United States Senator should be accepted as more valuable than the practical investigation of winds, currents, soundings and borings made by riparian experts and trained engineers. The people had asked for bread, and they had received a stone.

Up to this time the question had appeared but little in politics; but on the return of Mr. Gibbon and Mr. Patton, it was decided, that as the Congress was Democratic, it would be advisable to secure expressions from representative gatherings of that party in favor of the people's choice for a harbor site. The County Democratic Convention led the way, and was followed by the Congressional, District and State Conventions. Mr. Patton was nominated by the Democrats for Congress, and he began to tell the story of San Pedro at every campaign meeting in the district.

The Republican County Convention and Congressional District Convention adopted resolutions similar to those of the Democrats, and Mr. James McLachlan, who was nominated for Congress by the Republicans, announced himself for San Pedro as against any other location. Mr. McLachlan was elected. A Republican Legislature was chosen which elected George C. Perkins to the Senate to fill out Mr. Stanford's unexpired term.

An important newspaper change is to be noted as occurring in 1894. The Herald was sold, and passed into the hands of men who favored the San Pedro site. From that time forth it was an ardent advocate of that location, and in the winter of 1895 it did good service in gathering 20,000 names on a petition to Congress.

CHAPTER XIII.

THE FREE HARBOR LEAGUE.

THE period of the greatest discouragement for the advocates of San Pedro harbor came in the years 1894 and 1895, during the life of the 53rd Congress. The discovery which was made in July, 1894, that it was quite possible for Mr. Huntington to secure a majority in the congressional committees favoring his plan, in spite of the decision of the engineers against it, staggered the free harbor workers, whose fundamental doctrine had always been, that whatever might be done for San Pedro, appropriations for the other place were out of the range of possibility. Nevertheless, this was a period of comparative unanimity of sentiment in Los Angeles. People understood that it would be a long siege, and they settled down to it philosophically.

The Chamber of Commerce sent no delegate to the second session of the 53rd Congress, which took place in the winter and spring of 1895. Mr. Gibbon, who paid a visit to Washington at the opening of the session, reported that nothing was to be expected until a change was made in the personnel of the Senate Commerce Committee. The members of that committee having voted not to act until they had inspected the harbors, there was no hope for an appropriation until the visit was made or the committee changed.

An important piece of missionary work was, however, undertaken that winter, which served to keep the issue alive, both in Washington and in Los Angeles, and which led finally to the founding of a new organization, that was destined to play a most important part in the controversy. On the suggestion of E. A. Forrester, a member of the Board of Supervisors, a circular letter addressed to members of Congress was drawn up, describing the situation in most emphatic language, and a notice was then sent to each member of the Chamber of Commerce, asking him whether he had any friends among the members of the 53rd Congress. A printed list of the members of that Congress was enclosed. It was striking evidence of the cosmopolitan character of the city, that over 200 of the 600 members of the Chamber responded, and the Congressmen, whom they named, were almost from every State in the Union. More than two-thirds of the members of the Chamber had come to Los Angeles after they had reached mature years in some other portion of the Union, and the 53rd Congress was pretty well covered in the responses.

It was doubtless a matter of surprise to a member from some Ohio district, for example, to receive during that winter, a series of letters, one after another, from former fellow-townsmen, whose identity he had almost forgotten, all urging him to make a stand against an iniquitous scheme to "bottle up" the commercial privileges of Los Angeles in a harbor that was closed to competition. There was in each case a short personal letter and the circular.

The latter document used, as has been said, some very strong language, and when it was presented to the Directors of the Chamber, and was proposed to be sent out as an official document, objection was made on the ground that it was undiplomatic and quite out of keeping with the conservative attitude thus far taken by that body on the harbor issue.

The concluding paragraphs of the circular are fairly indicative of its general tenor, and they may be quoted:

> A situation so extraordinary and an injustice so long maintained calls at last for plain speech. The people of Southern California waited patiently during the first few years of this controversy, when it seemed that there might be an honest disagreement among the authorities, but now that the whole matter has been sifted to the bottom, and resolves itself into a question of how long a crafty corporation can defraud the people of their right to a free harbor, we shall hold back no longer, but call upon every lover of fair play to help us in this contest.
>
> The people of this section of California are gathered together from every point of the Union, few being natives of this State. Americans by birth and freeman by instinct, they refuse to submit to the commercial enthrallment which has so long retarded the growth and dwarfed the energies of San Francisco and Oakland. The presence of a competing railroad into Los Angeles has been thus far a protection against the encroachment of the Southern Pacific monopoly —but this will avail us but little if our water front is to be placed in their hands. We appeal, therefore, to our representatives at Washington—to all our representatives, in the sense that the whole Congress governs the whole nation—that those who are stealthily carrying forward this great wrong may be called to an open accounting, and that the rights of the people of the southwestern section of the Union may not be deliberately sacrificed to the private and personal interests of individuals, and the steady encroachment of a despotic corporation.

The document was finally sent out bearing the names of six well known citizens, who were designated as a "harbor committee." They were the following: John F. Humphreys, J. M. Elliott, W. D. Woolwine, J. R. Toberman, M. T. Collins and J. A. Pirtle.

Responses to this circular were numerous, and they revealed the fact that a great many members of Congress were fully awake to what was going on. Several explained the difficulty that must be met in any attempt to interfere with one item in a general appropriation bill, on the part of those who are not members of the House River and Harbor or the Senate Commerce Committees. These measures, it was said, are prepared in committee, and each member of the House or the Senate looks out for the particular items that concern his district. For him to interfere with any others would be entirely against precedent, and might result in his losing those in which he was directly interested. When the bill emerges into the general body, the great majority of the members are prepared to vote for it unchanged, fear-

L. W. BLINN.

ing lest, if amendments are attempted, the whole structure may topple over. In the House the bill is rushed through at a lightning rate of speed with no opportunity given for the considertion of special cases. The whole plan seemed admirably adapted, in fact, for putting through just such a plot as the one which the circular had outlined.

The Chamber of Commerce had by this time grown to be a large concern with many and varied interests, and while it still remained faithful to the San Pedro idea, it could not

FORMATION OF THE LEAGUE.

be expected to do the active fighting. The attitude taken by its officers in the matter of the circular to Congressmen, while it was accepted as entirely justifiable, led to the forming of a new organization, having for its one and only purpose the "securing of appropriations for a deep-water harbor at San Pedro, which will be accessible to as many railways as may seek to come to the water front." The name that was adopted was the "Free Harbor League," which constituted an argument in itself, or else, as its opponents claimed, a vicious begging of the whole question. Its first

FERD. K. RULE.

meetings were held during the month of October, 1895, at the Chamber of Commerce, and it made its headquarters there, throughout its career. Its original promoters were L. W. Blinn, John F. Francis, Chas. Weir, W. D. Woolwine, H. G. Otis, Chas. Forman, W. C. Patterson, Geo. W. Parsons, Robert McGarvin, Chas. Forrester, F. K. Rule, Geo. Gephard, W. H. Workman, Frank A. Gibson, J. M. Elliott, T. E. Gibbon, Harry E. Brook, C. D. Willard, H. Hawgood, H. T. Hazard, W. G. Kerckhoff, A. M. Stephens,

N. Bonfilio and W. B. Cline. In a short time the rolls contained the names of over 300 leading citizens, and the organization was ready for work.

L. W. Blinn, a lumber merchant, favorably known for his public-spirit was elected president, and W. D. Woolwine, a popular banker, was chosen secretary. The vice-presidents were Col. H. G. Otis and John F. Francis, and of the latter it may be said that he was, from the beginning, a most indefatigable worker in the cause — one of those who went

CHARLES WEIR.

right on with courage and cheerfulness when others were disheartened and ready to give up. To him fell the difficult and rather ungracious task of raising funds to carry on the work. In this he was assisted by Charles Weir; and together they labored assiduously until enough was secured to pay postage and printing expenses for the bureau of publicity which the League maintained, and also to pay—sometime later—the traveling expenses of several delegations sent on to Washington.

"When I had argued with a man for a quarter of an hour," said Mr. Francis, speaking afterwards of this work, "and succeeded at last in getting ten dollars out of him, it did look horribly small in comparison with the many millions that I knew Uncle Collis* had at his disposal; but I remembered that one dollar and the right were a whole lot bigger

GEORGE W. PARSONS.

than a million dollars and the wrong, and I took fresh courage and went to work again."

The general membership of the League was but seldom summoned together, and when it was, the fact must be recorded, that it pretty unanimously failed to appear. This led to no little sarcasm on the part of the Express, which was still an active Santa Monica advocate, and that paper declared that the League was a humbug, being a name and nothing more. This was hardly just—at least the failure of the members to attend the meetings proved nothing; for an

---

* Collis P. Huntington is generally called "Uncle Collis" by the people of the Pacific coast—a name which is not bestowed in ill-will but rather with friendly satire, for the reason—the present writer supposes—that he holds so large a section of the State of California in pawn.

executive committee had been chosen of men of character and ability and known experience in public work, and the members were satisfied—or seemed to be satisfied—that it would transact the League's business properly.

It must be admitted, however, that when the actual harbor campaign began, the League was steered and managed by a small clique of veteran San Pedro workers, and some of the taunts of the Express certainly struck home. The same criticism may be passed, however, on many public organizations. If the League had not been so well steered, it would not have passed so successfully the many reefs that lay waiting before it.

Early in 1896, Dr. Widney appeared before the Directors of the Chamber of Commerce, and narrated a conversation that he had recently had with Lieut-Col. W. H. H. Benyaurd, of the government engineers, who was thoroughly familiar with the conditions at San Pedro. Col. Benyaurd stated that he was about to send in a report to the Secretary of War with reference to the possibility of deepening the inner harbor of San Pedro from 14 to 18 feet* by a small amount of judicious dredging. Dr. Widney advised that Col. Benyaurd be questioned by the Chamber on this point, and that his forthcoming report be considered in formulating the Chamber's harbor policy for the winter's campaign.

In response to an inquiry from the chamber, Col. Benyaurd developed his project, which called for an expenditure of something under $400,000, and which would nearly double the efficiency of the inner harbor. It would not make a deep-sea harbor, for which 25 to 30 feet is required; but with 18 feet at low tide, a great many first-class ocean-going vessels could be accommodated.

The letter was put in the hands of the League managers, who gave it serious consideration; and at last a plan of action was evolved, somewhat different from that which had previously been pursued.

Senator White had written discouragingly of the situation at Washington, with regard to appropriations of every character. The treasury was drained of gold, and the balance between receipts and expenditures was heavily against

---
*All figures of harbor depth unless otherwise specified are for mean low tide.

the government. The Republican party had regained power in the House, and were bent on a policy of rigid economy. No money was to be spent on rivers and harbors, except for existing contracts and for emergencies. San Pedro's case would scarcely receive a decent hearing.

Representative McLachlan wrote in the same strain, and the friends of San Pedro from other States acquiesed in this view.

The suggestion of Col. Benyaurd seemed to have arrived pat on the moment. To ask for an appropriation for a deep-sea harbor at such a time was a waste of energy, and might be construed as unreasonable, and to the prejudice of the cause. Would it not be well, so the League committee argued, merely to ask for an appropriation for the inner harbor this year, and, while reaffirming confidence in the outer harbor plan, defer all action upon it until another year?

Against this it was argued that to lay aside the outer harbor demand might be construed as an abandonment of that part of the issue; but on the other side again it was said that, as there was not the slightest chance that anything could be done for Santa Monica in this session, the deep-water issue would not be broached at all, and could be taken up with renewed vigor next year, when the government was more disposed to consider harbor work. This additional argument was offered: that every dollar spent on the inside harbor helped to strengthen the government's interest in that port, rendering it less liable to be deserted for another.

One evening, when this topic was under informal discussion in a little gathering of League members, the suggestion was thrown out that perhaps Mr. Huntington was becoming quite as tired of the fight as the Los Angeles people were, and that an armistice for the season might appeal to him most favorably. One member of the party was delegated to investigate and find out how the land lay in that direction, he being on very good terms with one of Mr. Huntington's local representatives. When this representative was appealed to, he declared his belief that the Southern Pacific president would not only refrain from interfering with any attempt on the part of the League to secure an appropriation for San Pedro, in accordance with the Benyaurd project, but would even lend his powerful assistance. However, he would take the matter up with Mr. Huntington, and return an answer in two or three weeks.

In just about the time that is required to send a letter from Los Angeles to New York and get a response, the answer was given. Nobody was to be quoted as actually promising anything; it was all unofficial and confidential—but the League might go right ahead; the track was clear

---

CHAPTER XIV.

The Trap is Sprung.

WHETHER it would add materially to the interest of the story or not, it would certainly bring this narration better into line with dramatic unities, if it were possible to say that the armistice proposed by the League, and the seeming abandonment of the outer harbor idea, was nothing more nor less than a handsome piece of finesse, intended for the purpose of drawing Mr. Huntington's highest cards without showing San Pedro's hand in return; unfortunately, however, for the artistic quality of the harbor story, this was not the case. It was, after all, a chance shot that brought down the game. Regarded from the point of view of politics and warfare, the course adopted by the League was very near to a bad blunder. There was a time coming presently when the League was to be denounced by many of the old harbor workers, as a choice collection of mischief makers and simpletons. They had trusted a man, so the indictment against them went, who had repeatedly broken his promises before in the San Pedro matter, and who, from his record in all such transactions, was entitled to nobody's confidence. They had put a taint of insincerity into the whole San Pedro cause; they had offered to bargain away the old pledge of a "free harbor" for a few hundred thousands of immediate appropriation.

Finis coronat opus. It is the final outcome that tells the story. The League was damned most unanimously by the Santa Monica advocates, because it was for San Pedro, and it was damned again by the extremists of the San Pedro faction. As it is of a public man, so it is of a public organization: to be denounced by the partisans at each extreme is good evidence of a conservative policy that will win in the long run. If the League made a tactical error in compromising with Mr. Huntington, it certainly retrieved the mistake by a splendid showing of courage and clear sight later in the battle.

It is only fair to note, however, that the charge that Mr. Huntington broke his promise or acted treacherously in the affair is not in accord with the facts. To begin with, the understanding was informal and unofficial at both ends of the line, and the phraseology used was decidedly vague. There was no promise on Mr. Huntington's part that he would refrain from helping Santa Monica: only that he would not interfere with the efforts of the League to secure an appropriation for the inside harbor at San Pedro. Knowing the utterly demoralized condition of public finances, the members of the League never dreamed for one moment that Mr. Huntington could break into the treasury for a $3,000,000 appropriation; and no stipulation on that point was ever suggested. Nor is it entirely just to Mr. Huntington to say that he had previous to this time broken any pledges on the San Pedro harbor issue. Neither he nor any of his people had ever agreed in definite terms to abide by the decision of any of the various boards or commissions. Of course the appointment of a board—of several boards in fact—at the request of one of the parties to the controversy, certainly implies that all—and particularly that one—are to accept the result of the arbitration. There was something like a moral obligation—but no one expects corporations to be held by moral obligations, in a day when even legal obligations are scarcely kept inviolate.

The statement is sometimes made that there was a disposition on the part of the League to abandon the outer harbor, but this is not true. In all its resolutions, and in its memorial, which was addressed to Congress in February, 1896, the League declared its adherence to the idea of a deep-water harbor, and explained that it was only by reason of the depleted condition of the treasury that the request for an appropriation was limited to the interior work. The exact phraseology of the memorial is as follows: "At present the people of Southern California, recognizing that in the existing condition of the nation's finances, it would be very difficult to obtain an appropriation for the large amount necessary for a deep-water outer harbor, are confining their request to a moderate sum for the completion of work on the inner harbor. The object of the government engineers is to secure there a depth of eighteen feet."

The exact amount specified, under the Benyaurd estimate, is $392,725.

At a meeting of the League, February 7th, Col. H. G. Otis, Mr. W. G. Kerckhoff, Mr. W. C. Patterson and Mr. W. D. Woolwine were elected a special delegation to proceed to Washington in behalf of the League, and lay the San Pedro case before the River and Harbor Committee of the House.

Mr. James McLachlan, the member for the Sixth Congressional district—which under the reapportionment included Los Angeles county and a tier of coast counties running northward to Monterey—was an able lawyer, who had served as District Attorney, and had been actively identified with Republican politics in the southern part of the State for a number of years. He enjoyed, in a high degree, the confidence and good-will of his constituents, and his outlook for future political favors was excellent. The feeling was general in the district that great loss had already been suffered in the frequent changes of representatives, and Mr. McLachlan was regarded as a probable permanency. But the harbor question, which played havoc in so many directions, was destined to interfere most seriously with this plan.

The Chairman of the House Committee on Rivers and Harbors was Mr. Warren B. Hooker, of Fredonia, New York. He professed great interest in the San Pedro matter, and a time was set on the 17th of February for the hearing of the delegation. Mr. Binger Hermann, of Oregon, an influential member of the committee, and Chairman of the sub-committee on the Pacific Coast, showed much consideration to the League delegates, and on their departure assured them that he was confident their prayer would be granted.

Mr. McLachlan made the principal talk before the committee, and explained that, while there was no disposition on the part of the citizens of Los Angeles to abandon the idea of an outer deep-water harbor, it had been thought best, owing to the condition of the treasury, to ask only for the small appropriation for the Benyaurd project in the inner harbor. There was no Santa Monica-San Pedro discussion —the controversial features were ignored. The delegates were heard, and the committee took the matter under advisement.

Proceedings before the committees on the River and Harbor Bill are supposed to be entirely secret; nevertheless word was brought to Mr. McLachlan a few days later that Mr. Huntington had been before the Senate Commerce Committee in person and had put in a demand for $3,000,000 for Santa Monica.

"What does that mean?" Mr. McLachlan asked of several members of the committee. They seemed to regard it as a matter of no consequence. The demand for San Pedro had come from both Senators and all the representatives of the State, and was backed up by the representative commercial bodies, and was in accordance with the report of the engineering authorities of the government. The demand for Santa Monica was simply from Mr. Huntington. Moreover, the San Pedro amount was reasonable and possible, that for Santa Monica was preposterous and not to be considered.

Not entirely satisfied with the reasoning, and desirous of covering every loophole, Mr. McLachlan appealed directly to Mr. Hermann, and asked if anything was likely to be done for a deep-water harbor near Los Angeles. "If there is," said he, "the people of my district wish it to go to San Pedro."

To which Mr. Hermann returned answer that no appropriation would be made for an outside harbor that session. He was very clear and emphatic in his declaration.

Now, just about that same time Mr. Hermann was writing to Mr. Patterson the letter that revealed the whole plot. Evidently when Mr. Hermann wrote, March 16, 1896, he supposed that the bill would have emerged from the committee before the letter was received in Los Angeles. Some miscalculation with reference to a New England coast item made a temporary adjournment of the committee necessary, and the bill did not come before the House until April 6th.

Mr. Hermann's letter is such a politico-literary masterpiece, that it deserves to be reproduced in full:

Dear Mr. Patterson: Your much valued favor is at hand. I congratulate you on your safe arrival back to the land of sunshine and flowers, and to the bosom of your family.

I wish to express to you my deepest obligation for the honor you have done me in your Chillicothe interview, and in your Los Angeles interview. Your personal reference to myself convinces me that I possess your confidence and esteem. I shall endeavor in future acquaintance not to disappoint you. In one respect you shall not be deceived— I shall prove loyal to San Pedro Harbor. My position here since meeting yourself, Col. Otis and your other companions, has been directly at work to secure for San Pedro the recognition it merits. Your county should have both great works—San Pedro and Santa Monica—and later on as I so strongly suggested to you, a project for a still deeper draft should be insisted on for San Pedro. In this age of rivalry for deeper draft ships, and hence for correspondingly deeper water, no port can long retain its ascendancy, unless it constantly keeps in view the essential requisite of increasing its channel depths.

At this hour, I have succeeded in securing for San Pedro the contract system, which means the securing immediately of the entire $392,000 through contract, and the prompt completion of the whole project.

This is a great victory. Santa Monica secures the same advantage; the amount for completion, however, is much larger. We have placed about 25 of the important water ways of our nation under this system, and California receives two of these.

In three days we shall report our bill. Of course some event may happen by which we may suffer the loss of the items now contained in the bill, but I think we shall hold them. If one goes, the other must take the same course. I, for one, desire to bring to a close the antagonism between your two harbors, which has grown out of the apprehension that one place might be recognized by the government to the discrimination of the other. I wish that both shall have the same friendly treatment to the full extent of the maximum estimates for both.

As soon as I shall be permitted to give publicity to the

items of the bill, I shall be the first to telegraph Col. Otis of the result.

Again thanking you for your many kind attentions, and for the trouble taken in mailing me the newspapers with personal references, and in hopes that I shall have the pleasure of meeting and greeting you ere long under your own vine and fig tree, I am, with sincerest regards,

Sincerely yours,
BINGER HERMANN.

There is so much delicate humor in this production, that one is compelled to believe the Honorable Binger Hermann must have greatly enjoyed the process of inditing it. "In

W. D. WOOLWINE.

one respect you shall not be deceived," says he, mindful doubtless of the many conversations which he and Mr. Patterson had had, during which there was not a whisper of the possibility of giving a deep-water harbor to any place in the vicinity of Los Angeles. His exclusive reference to this "one respect" indicates that in Mr. Hermann's mind there was the thought of various *other* respects. "Of course," he observes with sinister suavity, "some event may happen by which we may suffer the loss of the items. If one goes the other must take the same course." Reading between the lines is here an easy task. Any protest against Mr. Huntington's plan meant for the people the loss of all they had asked.

Probably no letter, carried by the United States mail over the borders of Los Angeles county, ever brought a larger quantity of astonishment than this. Through the whole of the harbor discussion, there had been a few affable compromisers, who were in favor of "both harbors." Their theory of the proper thing to do was that the people should ask the government to build a deep-water harbor at Santa Monica because Mr. Huntington wished it there, and an another at San Pedro for competing commerce. These people were regarded as the prize idiots of the whole collection. To assume that the government would be willing even to consider the construction to two harbors within twenty miles of each other on a coast that had no harbors at all for 600 miles, for a scattered population of 200,000 people in a semi-desert and distant corner of the Union, was too preposterous to waste time in discussing. And yet, according to Mr. Hermann, the House Committee on Rivers and Harbors were prepared to take that step—if it could be done quietly and without objection. But if one item was thrown out, the other must go.

A meeting of the League was hastily summoned, and the Hermann letter was laid before the gathering. These men were not merely the representatives of a commercial interest, they were American citizens as well; and the enormity of the scheme in which they were asked to serve as partners struck them with horror. The thing seemed incredible, and some who were present declared that it was only a trick. Gen. Forman, for example, stated his belief that Mr. Hermann was merely "trying it on," to see how such a plan would be received. He called attention to the fact that the letter, which was now eight days old, stated the bill was to be reported in three days, while the dispatches from Washington showed that the bill was not reported, and was indeed not expected for another week. L. W. Blinn counseled moderation, lest precipitate action should destroy San Pedro's only hope. But Col. Otis, stung to anger by the deception that had been practiced upon the delegation, declared that the plot was evidently matured, and the League could not do less than to speak with frankness. The following resolutions were offered by him and adopted by a unanimous vote—so the League minutes state:

Resolved, By the Free Harbor League of Los Angeles, that we reaffirm our adherence to San Pedro as the true and proper site—as the people's as well as the government's site—for further harbor improvement, and that we are opposed to all legislation, if any such is contemplated by Congress, inconsistent with the purpose so supremely essential to the business interest and commercial advantage of Southern California.

In the meantime Mr. McLachlan, hearing a rumor that Santa Monica was to receive a deep-water harbor appropriation, had called upon the Chairman of the Committee, Mr. Hooker, and was by him assured that there was "nothing in it." But when the report was all ready for submission to the House, and was put in type at the government printing office, a correspondent of the San Francisco Examiner managed to secure proofs of the document, and in a few hours the schedule was spread by telegraph all over the country; and there were the two items in the list of continuing contracts: San Pedro $392,000 and Santa Monica $3,098,000. Almost at the same moment that he saw a copy of this list, Mr. McLachlan received a telegram from Mr. Patterson, informing him of what Mr. Hermann had written, and of the action of the League.

It was early in the morning, and the Los Angeles Congressman hurried to Mr. Hermann's residence. The Oregon man was just starting for the capitol, and they walked down the street together.

On the first mention of a Santa Monica appropriation, Mr. Hermann began to deny with some heat that any such grant was contemplated, whereupon Mr. McLachlan produced Mr. Patterson's telegram.

Finding that his scheme to keep the appropriation a secret, until it should be sprung in the House, had suffered defeat through his own premature betrayal of it, Mr. Hermann turned upon Mr. McLachlan in great wrath.

"Yes," he said, "we have given that money to Santa Monica, and we did not want anything said about it, for fear there might be an uproar, and both items would be knocked out. Now do you propose to make a fuss?"

Mr. McLachlan replied that he did.

"Well, you are by all odds the ———est fool that the whole —— —— State of California ever sent to Congress. Here you apply to us for an appropriation of $390,000 for your inside harbor at San Pedro, and you not only get that in full, but you get in addition over $3,000,000 more for Santa Monica, another place in your own district. There isn't a man in the whole House of Representatives that has had such handsome treatment. And here, instead of going down on your knees and thanking us, by ———, for giving you all you ask, and even more, you have the unspeakable effrontery to set up a roar."

"You don't understand the situation, Mr. Hermann," said the Los Angeles Congressman. "The people of my district will never consent—"

"The people of your district are a set of idiots that don't know when they are well off, if they can't take a double appropriation and two harbors, when they have only asked for one. All right," he continued, his voice rising higher as his anger grew, "both those items go out of the bill now, do you hear. If you won't take Santa Monica, you don't get San Pedro."

And true to his word, a few hours later, Mr. Binger Hermann rose in his place in the River and Harbor Committee, and, announcing that he had received several telegrams from Los Angeles, from the Free Harbor League and from citizens there, against the Santa Monica appropriation, and as the congressman from that district was opposed to that appropriation, he moved that all sums set aside for Los Angeles county be struck from the bill. The motion carried. Subsequently on the request of Charles A. Towne, a Minnesota representative, an appropriation of $50,000 for the dredging of the inner harbor at San Pedro was inserted, and in that shape the bill went to the House April 6, 1896.

CHAPTER XV.

THE DOUBLE APPROPRIATION SCHEME.

THE harbor issue had now shifted to a new phase. It was no longer a question of San Pedro or SantaMonica, but of a deep-sea harbor for Santa Monica and a small appropriation for interior work at San Pedro, or an alternative of nothing at all for either place. This proposition was so extraordinary and so unexpected, that it was not understood, in all its bearings, on its first presentation. The small contingent of perennial compromisers, who had insisted from the beginning that the government should be asked to construct both harbors, were promptly on hand with their "I told you so," and the Santa Monica sympathizers and the railway adherents were jubilant. But the average citizen, who had been disposed to favor San Pedro because it was the choice of the engineers, and to oppose the Port Los Angeles site, because he believed it to be entirely under Southern Pacific control, was staggered and dazed, and at first refused to believe.

The meeting of the League, when the Hermann letter was considered, took place March 28th. Six days later came a telegram from Representative McLachlan to Mr. Patterson, that placed the issue in plain and decided terms before the community. This telegram was as follows:

"Hermann requests me to notify Los Angeles Chamber of Commerce that if Los Angeles people will unite on schemes to complete inside harbor at San Pedro and construct deep-sea harbor at Santa Monica, with provision to admit all railroads to Santa Monica harbor over Southern Pacific tracks by paying pro rata cost, to be determined by Secretary of War, he believes an appropriation of $3,000,000 can be secured this session for said projects. To be effectual immediate action must be taken. I leave matter with you."

The proposition as to the admitting of other railways, on their payment of the pro rata of cost, was not new, for it had repeatedly been offered by the Southern Pacific, as an answer to the objection that Santa Monica was a monopoly harbor. On its face this seemed a fair enough proposition, but it was not acceptable to the San Pedro people, who declared that no plan could be devised that would, in the long run, protect another road that was entering the harbor over the Southern Pacific track and through that corporation's own land. A harbor with a free water front was better, so they asserted, than one where the rights of any other road than the one owning the adjacent territory could be maintained only by a constant appeal to the law, in courts where the Southern Pacific might perhaps have undue influence.

The offer from Mr. Hermann conveyed in his telegram did not differ materially, therefore, from what was darkly hinted in his letter to Mr. Patterson. It was interpreted by the members of the League to mean that Mr. Huntington had the House Committee so completely under his control that he could put in or take out appropriations to suit his whim, or could even use an offer of money for one place as a bribe to silence objection, while he got what he wished in another. Hence no help for a deep-sea harbor at San Pedro was to be expected from that committee.

There was another conclusion that was hastily reached by the League, as a result of the reception of the telegram. It was that Mr. McLachlan was no longer to be depended upon, as a friend of the "free harbor." If he had not gone completely over to the enemy, he must, at least, so the argument of the League members ran, have weakened and lost courage. A most unfortunate circumstance, which told against Mr. McLachlan in the judgment even of his friends, was that, while Mr. Patterson was reading the telegram which had just come from the office, he was accosted by a reporter from the Express, armed with a copy of Mr. McLachlan's message, which had been received some time before; and ere Mr. Patterson could leave his business office to go up to the Chamber of Commerce, he was called to the telephone by a delegation of Santa Monica residents, who began to talk of the telegram, and in response to a question from Mr. Patterson, they stated that a copy had been received some hours before by the Southern Pacific.

Mr. McLachlan offers what appears to be a fair explanation of all this, and the fact that he was to the end of the contest, a faithful supporter of the San Pedro deep-water plan, in spite of the division which afterwards seemed to take place in Los Angeles, certainly entitles him to the benefit of every doubt. Mr. McLachlan's account of the matter is as follows: After the River and Harbor Committee had stricken both items from the list, the $3,098,000 for Santa Monica and the $392,000 for San Pedro, Mr. Hermann sent for the Los Angeles Congressman and said to him: "Now we have fixed this, so that you can have several days' time in which to consult your people in Los Angeles. This is in effect a new issue, on which they have never expressed themselves to you. They favored San Pedro, as against Santa Monica; but now we are offering them both or neither. You have no right to decide so important a question, without listening to their views. Ask any of the older members, either in the House or Senate, and they will tell you you are crazy if you do so. The Chamber of Commerce is the representative body in Los Angeles; it does not stand for a special interest like that Free Harbor League; wire its president, and ask that a vote be taken. I know what their attitude will be on the choice between over $3,000,000 of money to be spent in their midst, or not a cent. I haven't served three terms of the River and Harbor Committee to learn nothing."

"You forget," said Mr. McLachlan, "that my people have repeatedly acted on the question of a deep-sea harbor at Santa Monica or San Pedro. This little appropriation for the San Pedro inner harbor cuts no figure in that issue."

"Wasn't that little appropriation, as you call it, all your people—your Free Harbor people—ever asked of us? However," continued Mr. Hermann, his wrath beginning to rise, "if you want to make a fool of yourself and all your constituents, it is no affair of mine. I have done my duty in the matter."

Full of doubt and apprehension, Mr. McLachlan went over to the Senate, and consulted with the two Senators from California. They both advised that Mr. Hermann's message be conveyed to the people of Los Angeles. It is, indeed, difficult to see how they could have advised otherwise. The people are not children, and they are entitled to know what is going on among their representatives, and to offer their views in the matter. As to whether their representatives are to be thereafter straightway bound by that expression is another question. The experiences of Mr. McLachlan and Senators White and Perkins in the harbor contest exemplify the difficulties that attend the setting up of any hard and fast rule. We may admit that the vox populi is the vox dei; but the question still remains open as to how the true vox populi is to be had. The public is in one respect like the monster that Stephano finds on Prospero's isle, in the "Tempest": it has more than one voice. And its utterance is not only discordant at times, but it varies as the days change. That there is such a thing as public sentiment, and that it does in the long run control politics and other human affairs, and that it ought to thus control, no one may doubt—but the representative who asks his constituents what they think on some particular question, and who expects to get back an answer within a few days that is a truthful expression of their views and more valuable than his own mature conclusions, is likely to receive a severe shock to his hopes.

Mr. McLachlan returned answer to Mr. Hermann that he would transmit his proposition to the Chamber of Commerce, and Mr. Hermann presumably told Mr. Huntington; for the Southern Pacific people in Los Angeles were in possession of the facts even before the telegram to Mr. Patterson had reached its destination. In order that both factions might be informed, Mr. McLachlan sent a copy of the telegram to Col. Osborne, the editor of the Express, and by some chance the duplicate arrived a few minutes before the original.

This was the incident which caused the Democrats to bestow upon Mr. McLachlan the sobriquet of "Telegraph Jim" in the campaign that presently followed, and which contributed in a large measure to his defeat then, and to his failure to secure a renomination two years later. That the railroad had nothing to do with Mr. McLachlan's mistake, if the telegram and his attitude at that time was a mistake, appears clear enough now that two campaigns have passed, during which he has had to contend with the active opposition of the railway adherents. It was his misfortune at the very threshold of his Congressional career to be flung up against one of the hardest problems that ever beset a Congressman. On one side lay huge appropriations for his district, and the favor of a powerful corporation, and on the other a return home with empty hands to a angry and discouraged constituency. The moral issues—if any such were involved—were indistinct and far removed. It may be easy now for us to decide what Mr. McLachlan should have done; it was

J. O. KOEPFLI.

not so easy then for him to determine, at each shifting phase of the situation, what was best to do. But, however good his intentions may have been, and however unjustly he may have been judged, the fact is that Mr. McLachlan's seat in Congress was sacrificed through his apparent vacillation on the harbor question in this eventful week.

A meeting of the directors of the Chamber took place on the day after the telegram was received. In the meantime, a special meeting of the League had been held and some resolutions adopted which were in the nature of a direct reply to Mr. Hermann's proposition. They set forth that if so large a sum was available for deep-water harbor improvement—which the League delegates had been heretofore assured was not the case—then it should be applied to the outer harbor at San Pedro, instead of to Mr. Huntington's private port of Santa Monica. When the directors of the Chamber met, Mr. J. O. Koepfli, who, besides being a member of that board, was also president of the Merchants Association, offered some emphatic resolutions covering the same ground as those passed by the League. A number of members of the Chamber were waiting in the anterooms to learn what action the board would take, and the threat was heard that if anything was done to interfere with the Santa Monica appropriation, a general meeting of the members would be summoned, just as in 1894. Desirous of avoiding this, which might at such a time of general excitement prove injurious both to the chamber and to the cause of San Pedro, Mr. Patterson advised a more moderate course. A brief resolution was framed, declaring that the chamber stood by its past record in favor of a deep-water harbor at San Pedro in preference to any other site. There was a sharp fight—for the "San Pedro or nothing" men, as they were called, were not disposed to yield; but the Koepfli resolution was voted down and the other passed.

When the news of the action of the board was conveyed to the ouside rooms, the Santa Monica adherents declared themselves dissatisfied with the so-called compromise, and promptly drew up and signed the petition for a general meeting. As the Washington dispatches indicated that the committee would report the bill within four days, the petition set a date for the meeting prior to that time, so that its decision could be conveyed to the House and perhaps affect the action of that body.

This new phase of the long harbor controversy, the "double appropriation" idea had roused the community of Los Angeles to the highest pitch of excitement. To one faction it represented the ruin of the hopes and efforts of many years; to another faction it was the fruition of all that had ever been dreamed; and to the great body of the people it was a new and complicated question on which they were asked to decide with most unseemly haste. The newspapers gave whole pages of space to the topic in every conceivable shape: telegrams from Washington, interviews with citizens, accounts of meetings, arguments for or against one site or the other, and fierce invectives against the railroad and its supporters, or against the folly of those who would throw away the proffered money. The uproar and confusion were so great, that for a time it was quite impossible to tell which side was in the ascendancy, but the fact that the proposed meeting of the Chamber was viewed with great apprehension by the San Pedro men, indicates that they felt none too sure of their ground. In the long run, when the sober, conscientious judgment of the people could be reached, they doubted not it would be recorded for the right, but they dreaded to think what this suddenly summoned meeting might bring forth.

However, their fears were superfluous, for when the call for the proposed meeting was sent out to the secretary of the Chamber, who happened at the time to be ill of a fever, he returned it with a letter calling attention to certain provisions of the constitution bearing on it, that would require several days for their fulfillment. In the meantime Congress would act. It was a mere technicality, that, like Mercutio's wound, was "neither as deep as a well nor as wide as a church door," but it served. The indignation of the petitioners was great; but the meeting never took place.

Public mass meetings were held, however, and resolutions were passed, representing both sides of the controversy. The San Pedro meeting was held out of doors, and was much larger than that held by the Santa Monica adherents in Illinois hall; but a number of substantial business men gave their names and their presence to the latter gathering. The division of the city was on the whole very nearly equal. If the San Pedro cause had the greater number, the Santa Monica side possessed seemingly the more powerful influence. The city council took action, and it was for the "double appropriation," and the Republican County convention, and also the Republican Congressional district convention that nominated Mr. McLachlan, passed resolutions in favor of all the appropriations that could be had, no matter what locality might receive them. The labor unions were all for San Pedro: at least the president and secretary of every union in Los Angeles signed telegrams to the California representatives, setting forth that the members of their respective organizations were opposed to the railroad and its proposed monopoly harbor. Petitions for and against the proposed "double harbor scheme" were circulated, and every citizen was forced to take a stand on one side or the other.

The work of circulating the petitions on the double harbor side fell into the hands of an employee of the Express, who hired several irresponsible individuals to gather names. One of the latter finally confessed that a large number of the signatures to the petitions were forgeries. The original petitions, which had been filed in Washington, were examined, and the statement was found to be true. The Express people disclaimed all knowledge of the transaction, and, indeed, the fact that among the forged names were many of the most prominent League members seemed to indicate that the work was that of some person of very limited intelligence.

The effect of this disclosure, however, was very bad on the "double harbor" cause, for it helped to a remarkable degree the formation of public sentiment against that side of the controversy. As time went on, particularly in the period between the action of the House, April 6th, and of the Senate, May 9th, the Santa Monica side lost, and the San Pedro side gained. This was due partly to the gradual awakening of the people to the full meaning of the attitude of the House Committee, and partly to the steady and effective work done by the agencies for influencing public opinion, the public bodies and the newspapers. It was a trying period, but Los Angeles stood the test well. The double harbor bribe had failed of its purpose.

CHAPTER XVI.

The Struggle in the Senate.

THE story of the consideration of the River and Harbor bill of 1896 by the House of Representatives may be written almost as easily as the treatise on snakes in Ireland. There was none. The bill was offered, and the motion was made for its adoption, under the suspension of the rules. Such a motion allows only forty minutes for debate, in one minute speeches, and a great part of that time is taken up by the reading of the bill. Mr. McLachlan was allowed one minute, in which time he made a vigorous objection, but without avail, to the treatment which his section had received. On the 6th of April, by a rising vote of 216 to 40, the bill passed the House and went up to the Senate—over $60,000,000 of public money ordered spent without fifteen minutes of discussion before the public! Of secret discussion and of consideration in committee there had been perhaps sufficient, if the negotiations carried on by Mr. Hermann were fair evidence of what that consideration was like.

On the 16th of April the Senate Committee on Commerce reached the San Pedro-Santa Monica matter and gave an audience to two delegations that had come on from Los Angeles to represent the conflicting interests. The Santa Monica, or "double harbor" delegation, as it preferred to be called, was made up of Mr. J. S. Slauson, who was a director in the Chamber of Commerce and a man of wealth and standing in the community, Mr. James B. Lankershim, a large property owner, and Mr. John W. Mitchell, an attorney who was active in Democratic politics, and ex-Senator Cornelius Cole. The Free Harbor League was represented by Mr. W. C. Patterson, Mr. Henry T. Hazard, Mr. Henry Hawgood, an engineer of high standing, and Judge Albert M. Stephens. Mr. Gibbon accompanied the latter party.

Considerable speculation was had over the probable attitude of Mr. McLachlan, for each delegation boasted that he was to appear before the Senate Committee in defense of its side of the case. Two letters from the representative to Col. Otis had been published, in which he had deplored the action of the League in opposing Santa Monica and had indicated a strong leaning toward the "double harbor" idea. He went into conference with both delegations, but kept his own counsel, until the hearing was about to begin, when he linked his arm into that of Mr Patterson, walked into the committee room, and seated himself with the Free Harbor men. Inasmuch as Mr. McLachlan's course in the harbor matter has been the subject of some little discussion in these pages, it is perhaps only just that we should reproduce here his concluding remarks before the Commerce Committee, and with these his connection with the case comes to an end.

"Afterwards, and before the River and Harbor bill was reported to the House, it was learned that the committee had put in the bill an appropriation for the full amount that was asked for the inside harbor at San Pedro, and had also included an appropriation (as we were credibly informed) of about $2,800,000 for the construction of an outside harbor at Santa Monica. I am bound here to state, as the Representative from that district, that I never asked for an appropriation for Santa Monica. We simply confined our efforts to the inside harbor at San Pedro. And I am in duty bound to say, as Representative from that district, coming fresh from the people, that I am not here to-day asking for an appropriation for Santa Monica, but that I am here asking for an appropriation to continue that inside harbor at San Pedro according to the plan of Colonel Benyaurd. And if in the wisdom of this committee it can see its way clear to give us an appropriation for an outside harbor, I am bound, under my pledges, to ask you to give that appropriation for the construction of the outside wall or breakwater at San Pedro."

His position came out even more clearly in the cross-examination, as follows:

Senator Elkins. You say that you appear here to get an appropriation for the inside harbor at San Pedro, and that you would like an appropriation for the outside harbor as well.

Mr. McLachlan. All the friends of San Pedro consider that on account of the economical tendency of this Congress, and on account of the condition of the Treasury, it would be wise to confine our efforts to getting an appropriation of $392,000 for the inside harbor; but since we discovered a disposition on the part of the House to give more to the vicinity of Los Angeles, I say, as a representative of that people coming here with those pledges, and that if there is to be an appropriation for an outer sea-wall, I ask it for the beginning of the outer harbor at San Pedro.

The Chairman. But you do not expect an appropriation of some $3,000,000 for Wilmington harbor provided the government continues to make a deep-sea harbor at San Pedro?

Mr. McLachlan. Yes; because we believe that one of the

most practical advantages to the deep-sea harbor will be the completion of the inside harbor at San Pedro.

The delegates made their presentation of the case, speaking in turn. Mr. Patterson dealt with the commercial features of the matter, Mr. Hawgood with the technical, and Mr. Hazard and Judge Stephens paid their respects to Mr. Huntington. The speakers on the other side deplored the attacks on Mr. Huntington, which they declared had their origin in mere prejudice, and said that the conservative, substantial people of Los Angeles were utterly indifferent what site was chosen for the harbor, provided it was built somewhere near that city.

There had been a great outcry among the party leaders and by the press of the country generally against the extravagance of the River and Harbor Bill, as it came from the House. It was supposed that the Senate would proceed to cut it down, and on that account no one, outside of the circle of Senators and Representatives who were engineering the scheme, had any idea that the $3,000,000 item would be restored either for Santa Monica or for San Pedro. Mr. White was hopeful that the $392,000 for the inner harbor at San Pedro might be put back in the bill, but even that was doubtful. It presently developed, however, that Mr. Huntington's influence in the Senate Committee on Commerce was quite as strong as it was in the House Committee on Rivers and Harbors, or that it covered at least a fair working majority. The expression "Mr. Huntington's influence" is used advisedly, for the official majority report of the committee practically admits that its action was based on that gentleman's views and wishes. To be sure, it does not call him by name, but the meaning is clear enough.

Nine members of the committee, under the leadership of Mr. Frye, the chairman, voted to restore the Santa Monica item of $3,098,000 to the bill; six voted against it, and of the latter two were opposed to giving so large an appropriation to any place in that vicinity, by reason of the depleted condition of public funds. Mr. White fought manfully against this proceeding, but to no avail. Argument was useless where votes were controlled by outside forces. At last, failing in his effort to divert the appropriation for a deep-sea harbor from Santa Monica to San Pedro, Mr. White proposed that a new commission should be appointed, and that its action should be made absolutely final by the device of appropriating the money in advance to go to whichever place should receive the decision. He appealed to the sense of fairness, to the honor and decency of the majority to grant this provision. "You cannot refuse so reasonable a demand," he said. But they did refuse. Their one and only purpose and desire was to give the appropriation to Mr. Huntington's site, and they were not to be turned aside by any form of argument or appeal.

When the bill emerged from the committee, it carried a majority and a minority report. The former was signed by the nine friends of Santa Monica. They were: Frye of Maine, Gorman of Maryland, Jones of Nevada, Elkins of West Virginia, Quay of Pennsylvania, Murphy of New York, McMillan of Michigan, McBride of Oregon and Squire of Wisconsin.

The majority report on the Santa Monica item was a brief document, containing about 150 words. It would seem that a proposition so extraordinary—the appropriation of so large a sum at such a time for a locality that had been ruled against by the engineering authorities of the government, and which was opposed by all the Representatives from the State, both the Senators and by nearly all the people of the adjacent district—called for a good deal of explaining, but the majority had very little to say. They could count the votes in the committee and Mr. Huntington's lobby assured them that a majority of the Senate could be relied upon, and they were content.

The report, therefore, merely states that a board had been appointed in 1891 which had reported in favor of San Pedro, and another in 1893, which had reported in favor of San Pedro. It then proceeds as follows, and this language which we quote constitutes practically all of the report:

> It was stoutly contended by persons having large interests in the commerce of the Pacific coast and familiar with the local conditions, that the opinion expressed by the board [of '93] was erroneous, that to act in accordance with it would be a waste of money; and in the River and Harbor

act of 1894 no appropriation for a harbor at either place was made.

While considering the bill herewith submitted, exhaustive hearings were given by your committee to parties representing both sides of this vexed question, including prominent engineers, both civil and military, and a conclusion was reached, in accordance with which a provision has been inserted for constructing a breakwater at Santa Monica.

These "exhaustive hearings" to which the committee refers and on which it proposed to discredit the judgment of the two boards of army engineers, based on months of study and research, consisted in a few speeches made by Los Angeles citizens, and the testimony of Messrs. Hood and Corthell, Southern Pacific engineers!

The minority report bore the names of Nelson of Minnesota, Caffery of Louisiana, Pasco of Florida, Vest of Missouri, Berry of Arkansas and White of California. It is a document which, if given in full, would consume one-third of this volume. It covers the ground thoroughly, showing the iniquity of the proposed appropriation, and supplying ample reasons why, if the money was to be spent, it should go to San Pedro.

When the item was reached in the Senate consideration of the report, which occurred May 8, 1896, Mr. White offered an amendment striking out the appropriation for Santa Monica and proposing instead the appropriation of $3,098,000 to go either to Santa Monica or to San Pedro, as might be decided by a special Board of Engineers, one of which Board should be an officer of the United States Navy, with a rank of not less than commander, to be appointed by the Secretary of the Navy, one a member of the Corps of Engineers of the United States Army, to be selected by the Secretary of War, and one a member of the Coast Geodetic Survey, to be selected by the Superintendent of the Survey. Provision was made by the amendment that if the decision went to Santa Monica:

"No expenditure of any part of the money hereby appropriated shall be made until the Southern Pacific Company, or the owner or owners thereof, shall execute an agreement and file the same with the Secretary of War that any railroad company may equally share with the said owner or owners in the use of the pier now constructed on the site of said harbor and the approaches thereto situated westerly of the easterly entrance to the Santa Monica tunnel upon paying its proportionate part of the cost of that portion of the same used by such railroad company and its proportionate part of the expense of maintenance of the particular part of said approaches and pier so used, to be determined by the Secretary of War in case of disagreement between the parties."

On this amendment Mr. White spoke, consuming such time as was allotted to the consideration of the River and Harbor Bill,. during the two days, May 9th and 10th. His speech began with the following sentences:

Mr. President, the question presented by the amendment which I have offered, and necessarily involved in the report of the committee, is of great local importance to those whom I in part represent, and it is of national importance on more than one account. In the first place, the United States are necessarily interested in everything pertaining to harbor improvements. This follows as a matter of course. Then the government is also interested in seeing that appropriations made by the Congress of the United States by means of a River and Harbor bill are made for public purposes, and that the diversion of the funds of the government is not accomplished through private channels or for personal ends.

The Senator then displayed maps of the two harbors and the surrounding country, and gave a complete description of their physical features. He then stated the issue as follows:

The questions before the Senate may be summarized thus: First, is it necessary that we should have an outer harbor at all? Second, if so, should that outer harbor be located at San Pedro or should it be fixed at Santa Monica?

Mr. President, if it be conceded that the selection at San Pedro, as contended by my distinguished nautical friend the chairman of the committee [Mr. Frye], is not well located, and that the government is not warranted in making the expenditure at that point, the question still remains, will the government be justified in making the expenditure at the point designated in the bill?

Mr. White then told of the appointment of the two boards of 1891 and 1893, and summarized their reports. This brought him to the existing situation with reference to the $3,000,000 appropriation, which he handled as follows:

> I wish to call the attention of the Senate to what I consider an extraordinary feature of the case—a peculiar feature of the controversy. It is and would be in any instance rather singular that the Congress of the United States should find it necessary to make an appropriation of public money in the face of the desire of local representatives, and it is almost impossible that such a condition of things can ever exist unless there is some uncommon influence not usually applicable and not generally brought into exercise.
>
> Let us examine this situation. In the report of the committee, from which I have read the general synopsis, we find the following:
>
> "It was stoutly contended by persons having large interests in the commerce of the Pacific coast and familiar with the local conditions that the opinion expressed by the board was erroneous; that to act in accordance with it would be a waste of money."
>
> The opinions thus expressed were the expressions of the Southern Pacific Railroad Company, and that persistency which has been referred to has been and is the persistency, the potential persistency, of that company. I recognize the right of every man to proceed upon proper lines to gain all grants from Congress which his eloquence and skill, his arguments and persuasion, may be able to obtain, but I do not recognize the right of such person to control me without some argument demonstrating that the appropriation of this large amount of money in defiance of official recommendation is for the public interest.
>
> Let me go a step further in the history of this matter. I desire the Senate and every member of it to understand the situation, and so understanding it, if members of this body are willing to take the responsibility of voting away $3,098,000 it is their affair, not mine. But I shall give the facts as I know them, and I shall state nothing that I do not believe to be true, and I shall gladly correct any statements which I may discover to be unfounded.
>
> When the present Congress convened, the situation of this matter was briefly as I shall state it. Nothing had been done upon the report of the Board of Engineers and no appropriation had been made. In the meantime Colonel Benyaurd had devised the project for the improvement of the inner harbor to which I have referred. I called for that

project, which was filed away in the War Department by resolution which passed the Senate at the close of the last session. The report of Colonel Benyaurd was thereafter incorporated in the official records of the Chief of Engineers, and when the River and Harbor bill came before the committee of the House for consideration, I appeared there and so also did my colleague, and the distinguished member of the House already referred to was likewise there. We presented our claims for the further improvement of the inner harbor at San Pedro or Wilmington—I use the words indiscriminately—the Benyaurd project, against which there was, so far as we knew or now know, no disclosed objection.

I stated there, as others did, that in view of the depleted condition of the Treasury, and because we deemed it wholly unlikely that Congress would care to embark in so expensive a work as a three-million-dollar outer harbor at this time, we should be satisfied if we were given a continuing contract for the inner harbor at San Pedro, involving the $392,000. We left. Nothing more was heard by me of this affair until I learned indirectly that a provision had been printed in the draft of the river and harbor bill for two million eight hundred and odd thousand dollars for a harbor at Santa Monica or Port Los Angeles, and that $392,000 had also, it was rumored, been appropriated for San Pedro.

Thus I discovered that to some extent my State occupied a higher plane than that upon which other Commonwealths have been in the habit of treading; that while there were some who were forced to solicit appropriations and to make arguments to obtain the same, in my instance such favors came not only unsolicited but unwanted.

Mr. Gray. Thrust on you.

Mr. White. However, a great local disturbance arose in Los Angeles. As shown by the hearings printed by the Committee on Commerce, a telegram was sent to Los Angeles stating that if the people there would unite they could have the inner harbor at San Pedro, but they must take it with the outer harbor at Santa Monica.

Mr. George. Who sent that telegram?

Mr. White. The Representative. I will refer to the page in a moment. The result of it all was that the River and Harbor Committee dropped the whole matter, leaving only an appropriation of $50,000 for the inner harbor at San Pedro on the Benyaurd proposition and no continuing contract at all. Indeed, my State was not honored with any continuing contract in the bill as it came to this end of the

Capitol. When the measure reached the Committee on Commerce the fight was renewed.

I neglected to say that the River and Harbor Committee had the benefit (not in my presence, however) of the testimony of Messrs. Corthell and Hood, whose views have been published by the House. The combat was thence transferred to the Senate. Upon a day fixed by common consent representatives from the State of California were brought here, business men, persons of standing and integrity, who represented both sides of the question. Some of those gentlemen (and their evidence is in the hearings here) argued in favor of Santa Monica and some in favor of San Pedro.

Petitions were filed; telegrams without number were recived. One of my constituents stated to me, "Let us have the appropriation, even if it is to go to Arroyo Seco," which means "dry creek." The impression prevailed in the community that there was an opportunity to get $3,000,000, and some thought it was useless to longer make a fight for San Pedro, where the vast majority of the people wanted the harbor Sooner than lose the appropriation for the inner harbor, and this large amount of money promised to be disbursed in the locality, they were willing to locate a harbor anywhere.

Of course that did not represent the universal sentiment. I may say the record here shows a telegram signed by some two or three hundred of the leading business men of Los Angeles insisting upon my advocacy of both appropriations for San Pedro. But if I had not received that telegram I should not have changed my position. It cannot alter my attitude standing here in the discharge of a public duty merely because a vote of mine is to prevent the expenditure of money in my locality. If I know that the expenditure is not to be made in the public interest—that it is sought for a private purpose—I will not vote for it. Were I outside of official life, selfishness, which dominates many of us, and to some extent influences us all, might perhaps lead me to applaud an act which would involve local disbursement of such an elaborate sum. But I could not find myself authorized, and do not deem myself empowered, to appropriate one cent unless I find it to be for a public purpose and for the public interest.

Mr. White then took up the question of the holding ground at San Pedro, and showed by the testimony of over forty ship masters the fallacy of the objections that had been urged by Mr. Hood and Mr. Huntington. He discussed at some length the monopoly feature of the Santa Monica site, showing the difficulty that would beset other roads than the Southern Pacific, seeking an entrance to that harbor. He also answered Mr. Corthell's theory of the littoral currents, commenting quizzically on the intelligent discrimination of a current which would carry sand to the west while it carried lumber, coal and dead bodies to the east. The concluding paragraphs of his speech are as follows:

Mr. President, what is the amendment which I have introduced and upon which I ask a vote? What is the proposition which I make to the Senate regarding the subject? The gist of the matter is the making of an appropriation and the expenditure of the money at either San Pedro or Port Los Angeles, the location to be determined by a board consisting of an officer of the United States Navy, of rank not less than commander, to be appointed by the Secretary of the Navy; a member of the Corps of Engineers of the United States Army, to be selected by the Secretary of War, and a member of the Coast and Geodetic Survey, to be selected by the Superintendent of the Survey.

Now, I ask those who are disposed to be fair, who wish this important subject determined accurately, what objection can be rationally made to this plan. An objection might, indeed, be urged upon the part of those who advocate San Pedro and who are interested on the part of the government in the disbursement of public moneys, upon the ground that two boards have already reported against Santa Monica, and therefore it may be said that we are going too far in selecting a third tribunal when we have two positive reports made by competent persons. In offering the amendment I do not in the slightest degree impugn the motive, question the integrity, or doubt the capacity of the eight distinguished gentlemen who have passed upon this subject. I believe that as to the location of the harbor their views are correct. I have entire confidence in the accuracy of their positions, but a majority of the Commerce Committee and several Senators who affirm that they have thought about this subject for seven or eight years announce that the engineers are wrong; that the boards are mistaken; that these eight impartial, honest servants of the government are all misinformed; that among these eight scientific men of integrity there was not one competent to pass judgment or able to reach the true conclusion.

Let me ask those who oppose my view, why object to the appointment of a skilled and unbiased commission to pass upon the subject? If he be not satisfied with that which has been done, if it be contended that the action of previous boards must be disregarded, can we not find some one somewhere to whom we will be willing to commit this subject? Will Senators who have no more knowledge of the situation than that derived from the cursory and scattered hearings before the committee pretend to tell me that they know absolutely and conclusively that these eight officers of the government were wrong, and that they are so satisfied of this that they want no more light; that the glorious radiance flashing from the information which they have received here renders the advent of other knowledge impossible? That the limit of intellectual absorption has been attained? Is this the position? Will anyone admit that he is unwilling to lay this matter before a competent, impartial board? Yes; the advocates of Santa Monica must so concede. They will not consent to the submission of their pretensions to any person or officer. They say in effect by this refusal that no board will report in favor of their location. They decline to submit their arguments to competent scrutiny. Why? Not because they think their success possible. They would not then refuse. They decline, because—and there is no other deduction possible from their conduct—they know that no impartial and competent tribunal will decide in their favor. They fear fairness.

Is the constitution of the proposed board objected to? If so, why not suggest improvement? I and those who are contending in conjunction with me are prepared to do that which is honest and equitable. Is it possible to form any commission to constitute any board to which the majority of the committee will be willing to submit? Evidently it is not possible. Mr. President, you cannot find, you cannot devise, you cannot suggest any tribunal, any board, any committee, any qualified person or persons to whom this discretion will be committed by my friends of the opposition. They rest in security upon the theory that Senators are ready to vote against the report of the government engineers and against everything official, are willing to appropriate in the face of authoritative condemnation, and they do not therefore propose to risk any board.

> You refuse to recommit for examination; you decline to subject it to candid investigation, but it is proposed to boldly overturn and cast aside the suggestions of those to whose recommendation we should at least award decent consideration, and to substitute therefor the conclusions of employees of Mr. Huntington and to enable them to place at his feet a great winning made from the government of the United States.
>
> If the advocates of Santa Monica believe that they have the meritorious side, then let them face a commission chosen upon impartial lines. With the judgment of such a board I shall be content. Until some fair, competent, and disinterested man, appointed according to law, has determined that this appropriation is justifiable, I shall continue to oppose it and raise my voice against it, even though I stand alone.

Senator Berry followed Mr. White in a strong speech, devoted mainly to the expenditure of government money in behalf of a private interest without warrant from the engineering authorities. Senator Vest spoke, defining his position, which was in opposition to so large an appropriation at that time for either site. Senator Perkins delivered an effective address, dealing with the navigation questions that were involved, on which he was specially competent to speak by reason of wide acquaintance with the topic and a long personal experience as a ship master on the Pacific Coast. His plea for San Pedro carried great weight.

The only speaker on the Santa Monica side was Mr. Frye, although Senator Stewart of Nevada, in his cross-questioning of Mr. Perkins, gave some aid to that cause.

Senator Frye's speech occupied the greater part of a day, and was an able presentation of a rather awkward case. The following passages will give some idea of the tenor of his argument:

> Here (indicating the Port Los Angeles location on the map) is the proposed breakwater to protect the ships in the inside. It is about a mile and one-third from the shore. It is about 8,400 feet long. It includes inside of it an area of about 555 acres of deep water, which will accommodate about 222 deep draft vessels at anchor. Every inch inside is excellent holding ground, being mud and gravel. It is absolutely protected by a range of mountains over a thousand feet high from the north winds, the northeast and the north-

west winds. It is absolutely protected on the other side by the highlands from every southeast wind. The dangerous wind of the Pacific coast is that from the southeast. There is no great fear of the other, except occasionally a heavy southwest gale. This bay is absolutely protected from everything except the southwest wave line, as it is called, and the westerly winds. . . .

Somebody wished to know where you could place the wharf in San Pedro, and I assure the Senators it is a very

SENATOR GEORGE C. PERKINS.

serious question. Here is the Southern Pacific railroad, "that horrible instrument of injury to the country," running right along here and out to this point (indicating). This is a very high bluff (indicating), I should say 60 or 70 feet high, rocky and perpendicular. The waves of the ocean are nearly all the time dashing up against it at the foot. Where are you going to put your wharves? Where will you locate them? The second Board of Engineers said that you could make a dozen in some way or other—it would be very expensive for this railroad—by running your railroad out on the breakwater, and then attaching your wharves to it.

Now, is not that conclusive proof that the second board did not know that the southwest wave line accompanied a southeast shore wind? Have not Senators here seen the power of waves on the Pacific when they came sweeping in across the sea over water that is 300 fathoms deep within three miles from the shore and strike that breakwater 10 feet up out of the water? How long would a railroad track stand on the top of that breakwater? How long would a ship lying by the wharves stay there? Those waves would break over that breakwater from 40 to 50 feet high, and, as a woman would sweep with a broom the dust from the ground, sweep away your railroads and your railroad tracks and completely submerge every vessel lying by the wharves attached to the breakwater. . . . .

Now, to a certain extent this is a railroad fight. The Senator from Arkansas (Mr. Berry) thinks it is a fearful thing for a Senator to be on the side of a great railroad and a "greedy monopoly." I have never seen anything more greedy in my experience than this little Terminal railroad. It is about 40 miles long. What is it there for? It was built there after the first report of the Board of Engineers. Under the first report of the Board of Engineers there were certain gentlemen who thought they saw a chance for a speculation. . . . .

There is room at Santa Monica for twelve tracks, for ten more tracks. Any other railroad can get in just as easily as the Southern Pacific Company did. Mr. Huntington said he would build the tracks for them for $10,000 a mile, and this bill provides that they should use his wharf if they desire to do so. . . . .

We have heard talk about corruption and bribery, but in this there is more bribery from the good feeling which exists between Senators than from any and every other cause known to man. I think that we yield our preferences and our wishes to Senators when no amount of money and no amount of honor would induce us to do it under any circumstances, and I admit that I am one of the yielding kind, for while it has been charged in Los Angeles that I am owned by the Southern Pacific Railroad I would rather have the kindly regard of these Senators I am addressing, and their confidence, than the support of all the railroads and railroad magnates on the face of the earth, and all the money that all of them possess. The Examiner said that if I succeeded in getting Santa Monica adopted as a harbor my pockets would be lined with gold, a happy way they have of talking about public men, sir, in your State, Mr. White; pleasant and agreeable compliments they pay us—a high estimate they make of us. . . . .

In my experience with river and harbor bills, wherever a majority of the committee wish to overrule the army engineers, that majority does it without the slightest compunction of conscience.

A board of army engineers made its report, and I declare that never in a single instance did the first board of army engineers or the second board of army engineers, either one of them, condemn Santa Monica as a harbor, and no condemnation of it can be found in their report. They simply expressed a preference for San Pedro and gave their reasons, and the most prominent reason was that it was better adapted to fortifications than was Santa Monica. . . . . .

When the report was made to us in our Committee of Commerce, we considered the matter, and determined not to appropriate for a harbor at San Pedro at that time. Shortly afterwards I went out there. Now, the Senator from California [Mr. White] alluded to the "distinguished navigator from Maine," and his visit to San Pedro somewhat sarcastically; but I'll forgive him. I will say, nevertheless, I went out there. I do know something about harbors. I have common sense, I think; what they call in New England "horse sense"; and I have looked over a great many harbors in my life. I am able to form a general judgment. I think I could tell, looking at that picture (indicating), which was the better place for a harbor; and I pity the Senator who could not. I went down there on that bluff (indicating) at San Pedro.

Who took me there? The Southern Pacific owned me then, of course, because the president of the Southern Pacific railroad took me there, and he had about a dozen of his Southern Pacific officers with him. Senator Stanford was urging the necessity of an appropriation, stating that it was vital to their railroad, that it was vital to the interests of commerce, that a great commerce would spring up there if they only had a safe harbor. I stood on that bluff (indicating), about seventy feet high, the bluff running down straight, rocky, and looked out into this proposed harbor. About the first question I asked the Senator—there was only a slight breeze blowing that was southerly, and the little waves were rushing up against the rocky side of this bluff upon which I stood—I asked the Senator which was the troublesome wind there. He said it was the southeasterly wind. "If your bad wind is the southeasterly wind," I said, "Senator, how is that harbor, which looks right into the southeast, going to be protected? How are ships going to be protected? Where are you going to put your wharf?" He said they were going to put a wharf—Senators can perhaps see the little point running out there about half an inch along the right side of that picture (indicating)—there, inside of that breakwater. "But," said I, "my dear Senator, that wharf will not stay there at all. The southeast wind will take that wharf off"—Senators can see the line there (indicating)—"and any vessel that lies there."

Shortly afterwards they went to work on that wharf. They spent several hundred thousand dollars in building it, and got it out perhaps a hundred or a hundred and fifty feet, when they concluded that it was money thrown away and gave it up. Whether I am a "navigator" or not, I made up my mind very deliberately then that a safe harbor at San Pedro was an impossibility on account of the southeast winds. . . . .

The next day I went up to Santa Monica; I think it was Saturday; and for two days I enjoyed the gracious hospitality of one of the pleasantest homes which I ever visited in my life. The host was so much of a gentleman that he never mentioned harbor to me. But on Sunday, having nothing to do, I went prospecting on harbor business. I looked off onto Santa Monica bay right from a high bluff; right up here (indicating). Here is Santa Monica. I was right here on this bluff, and looked out into this beautiful bay. It was a still day, and the bay looked like a lake. I thought I never had seen in my life a better place made by the Almighty for a harbor than that was. It seemed to be absolutely perfect. No northeast wind, no north wind, no southeast wind, no southwest wind could touch it; it was a remarkably well-protected resting-place, and it did not need a great expenditure to make it absolutely safe, so it seemed to me. I have never divested myself of that first opinion, which I formed then, notwithstanding the reports of two boards of army engineers; and the other board, which is proposed now, if it should come to the same conclusion, would leave me in precisely the same spot. That may seem like obstinacy, but it is a deep, well-fixed judgment of my own.

Mr. White's reply was filled with good-natured satire on the attitude taken by Senator Frye as an authority on navigation and harbor engineering:

The Senator from Maine, while disclaiming engineering attainments, seems to think that I was reflecting up on him in some way when I spoke of him as a navigator. I did think that the Senator from Maine was possessed of much nautical knowledge; but if I was in error I will withdraw the remark. [Laughter.] But while the Senator from Maine disclaims familiarity with technical matters he informs us that anyone can see the conclusive merits of his argument by a mere glance at his map. Those of the most ordinary intellectual development must see that he is right. This is his faith, and he does not hesitate to set up his nonprofessional judgment against those who have been employed by the government to pass upon this subject. He not only relies upon himself against skilled authority, but he tells us that as there is one chance in ten of a decision in favor of San Pedro he will vote against the amendment which I offer. This is more conciliation.

Mr. President, the amendment which I have advocated involves the appointing of a commission of admittedly unbiased and impartial men to determine between these two locations—San Pedro and Santa Monica. What is the objection to this? The Senator from Maine says that possibly there might be a decision for San Pedro—only one chance out of ten, he declares. But this is quite enough. No impartial experts who choose San Pedro can, according to his view, be relied on. No impartial or other board for him. What does he want? He demands the power to personally solve this dispute his own way.

The struggle which I have made here may seem stubborn to some, but it is maintained in the consciousness and belief that I am acting for the public interest. No demagogical appeal—notwithstanding intimations to the contrary—has influenced or ever will influence me. I have been as able as the Senator from Maine to maintain myself in my conservative methods without condescending to belittlement. I experience natural pride in my presence here, but I would willingly sacrifice that honor rather than yield my maturely formed judgment to any senseless clamor, to threats or flattery, to condemnation or applause, and I might say, Mr. President, that I would rather be a lawyer whose word was as good as the rich man's bond, and whose opinion upon an intricate question of judicial science was valued by the master minds of my profession, than to hold in my hand all the honors that ever were won by appeals to the passions and prejudices of men.

UNCLE COLLIS MEETS AN OBSTACLE.
(Cartoon in the "Times", March, 1896.)

As the debate progressed, occupying almost the entire time of the Senate for five days of a busy session, a great deal of space was given to the Santa Monica-San Pedro topic by the newspapers. The leading journals of the country discussed the issue editorially, and it may be added that they were unanimously on the San Pedro side. Many of the correspondents took an active personal interest in the fight— Van Alstine, Bierce, Brown, Wellman, McLeod and others— and their reports were most effective in holding indifferent votes in line and demoralizing the Santa Monica end of the contest. Senators of the United States are very great men, but they nevertheless read pretty carefully the utterances of the leading newspapers, and seriously incline toward their views. Every day of the debate strengthened the San Pedro line, because in the opinion of the public generally that side was right and the other wrong. At last the pressure came too strong even for Mr. Frye. Mr. White's repeated taunt, that he dare not refer the question to a competent, unprejudiced board, struck home. There were frequent conferences between the Senator from Maine and Mr. Huntington. As various forms of compromises were considered in the committee Mr. Frye went back and forth, consulting first with Mr. Huntington ("your principal," as Mr. White spoke of him to the Maine Senator with some contempt, and the latter did not resent it) and then with the committee, until at last an amendment was passed, which was acceptable to all concerned. This called for the appointment of a board of five engineers, one from the Navy, one from the Coast and Geodetic Survey, and three from civil life, to be named by the President. The $392,000 for a continuing contract for San Pedro was restored to the bill, of which $100,000 was appropriated for immediate use.

The bill then passed to conference, where it encountered the unfriendly inspection of Mr. Hermann, who at first positively refused to accept the proposed compromise. Possibly Mr. Huntington had changed his mind about the measure, and had decided to oppose it, even after Mr. Frye had put it forward with his authority, or perhaps Mr. Hermann was proceeding on his own volition to stand out against any plan that might at last give the money to San Pedro. It was just at the end of the session. Both Houses had completed their work, and were waiting for the report of the conferees. Several days passed, Congress meeting each day and adjourning over to the next. At last it began to leak out that it was the Santa Monica-San Pedro item which was causing all the delay, and that strenuous efforts were being put forth by Mr. Hermann to have it thrown out of the bill entirely. Whereupon Representative James G. Maguire, of San Francisco, who had been an uncompromising friend of San Pedro from the very beginning, went to the members of the committee and threatened to call the matter up in the House the next day, and expose what was going on, unless the compromise was allowed to stand. This brought Mr. Hermann to terms, and the bill was reported unchanged, except for a provision that if the deep-water harbor went to San Pedro by the decision of the Board, the $392,000 was not to be spent there. In this form the bill passed both Houses. It was vetoed by President Cleveland, on the ground that the treasury was not prepared to meet such enormous expenditures, but was promptly passed over his veto and became a law.

CHAPTER XVII.

ONE MORE FINAL DECISION.

THERE was great rejoicing in Los Angeles when the news came of the passage of the River and Harbor Bill containing the deep-water harbor appropriation, and the provision for the appointment of a Board to designate where the work should be done.* When Senator White returned home a few weeks later, a special train went out to meet him containing several hundred of his friends and admirers. The cars were decorated with flags and flowers, and as the train passed through the neighboring cities great crowds were gathered at the station to cheer the man who had made a brave fight for the people, for so it was regarded. At Los Angeles a parade was formed to act as Mr. White's escort from the depot to a place where a public reception was to take place. There was no element of political partisanship in the gathering—indeed, Republicans were more numerous and active than Democrats.

It might be well to add in this connection that when Senator Perkins visited Los Angeles some months later, although it was in the midst of a Presidential campaign and his mission was to make a political speech on the Republican side, a similar reception was tendered him, and in this

---

* For full text of the law, see Appendix.

the Democrats were given a chance to reciprocate, and they accepted it handsomely. The issue which had so long divided the people of Los Angeles was in no sense a political one, and the conflict had been so fierce and so determined that an ordinary Presidential campaign seemed almost tame in comparison.

It was a curious and perhaps significant fact that the rejoicing at the outcome was chiefly from the San Pedro side. For the fourth time now, the matter of the harbor location had been submitted to a commission for "final" settlement. When Gen. Alexander and Col. Mendell had looked the ground over in 1869, before the government had expended one dollar on a harbor for Los Angeles, they selected San Pedro. Twenty-one years later they were followed by a Board, consisting of the army engineers, Mendell, Gillespie and Benyaurd, who returned the same verdict. Then came a few years after the Craighill Board with the same decision, and now that a fourth body was to go over the ground the people made no question that the result would be the same—another finding for San Pedro. There was this difference, however, between the new Board and its predecessors; the latter had been appointed to decide on a location for which Congress might or might not make the necessary appropriation; but the Board that was now to be named had the money already in hand, and was merely to designate where it was to be spent. It seemed reasonably certain that this was a form of decision that must actually decide.

There were plenty of doubters, however. "Uncle will contrive some way to open it up again," said they. "He never would have accepted the compromise, unless there was a joker in it. White is a clever fellow, but the Southern Pacific has overreached him, as it does everybody." A year later, when Secretary of War Alger succeeded in hanging up the appropriation for nine months, these people made the most of their chance to say, "I told you so."

A more serious cause for question lay in the possible appointment on the Board of men who might be influenced by other considerations than those of the real merit of the contending sites. It was evident that the appointees must be men of the highest character and standing, to avoid the chance for scandal. An appropriation of $50,000, or such part as might be needed, for the expenses of the Board, made it possible to secure men of eminence in the profession to fill the places that were open to engineers from private life. It is difficult, perhaps impossible, for a man to attain high rank in that profession without the possession of a correspondingly high character; and there was good reason to believe that the men who were chosen would be above reproach.

The bill passed early in June, 1896, and the appointments were made in the following October. These were: From the navy, Rear Admiral John G. Walker; from the coast survey, Augustus F. Rodgers, and from civil life, appointed by President Cleveland, William H. Burr, George S. Morrison and Richard P. Morgan.

These appointments were all—save one—received with satisfaction and confidence. Rear Admiral Walker, who was chairman of the Board, was a man of mature years, with wide experience in navigation matters, and his character was above possible question. He has since then served with distinction at the head of the commission appointed by Congress to report on the Nicaragua canal project. His name, serving as the title of the board that was now to settle the question of Santa Monica or San Pedro, once and for all, was in itself almost a guarantee that the decision would be just and honorable. Of Professor Rodgers, the representative of the Coast Survey, and of Messrs. Morrison and Burr, nothing but favorable reports were heard. Each stood well in his profession and was believed to be incorruptible. But the last name, Richard Price Morgan, was received with doubt and surprise. It was known that he had at one time done the Southern Pacific an important service, and that his son was now in the employ of that road. There were also other objections to him, offered by those who professed to be familiar with his career. A protest was at once filed with President Cleveland by Senator White, who declared the appointment to be entirely unsuitable. Mr. Cleveland then addressed a letter to Mr. Morgan, and it is said by those who have seen a copy of the letter that it was plainly intended to "draw" the latter's resignation, or in the event that it failed of that purpose, to give him to understand the nature of the doubts regarding him, and to put him, so to speak, on his best behavior. Mr. Morgan did not resign, but served with the Board. He did not live at the same hotel with the other members, however, nor go with them on any of the little pleasure trips which they took about the country, during their leisure, nor did he fraternize with them —or shall we say they with him?—in any way. In the end, he brought in a minority report, containing some very peculiar matter.

The public sessions of the Walker Board, at the Chamber of Commerce, began December 21, 1896, and lasted through seven days. Prior to that time the Board had spent some weeks studying the technical features of the question, from charts and maps and other data of the Coast Survey. The "Gedney" of the Coast Survey was placed at their disposal by the government, and two months were spent in a thorough, practical investigation of the harbor sites. All soundings were taken anew and fresh charts were prepared. Borings were made all along the lines of the proposed breakwaters and at intervals through the harbors. Faithful and thorough work was done, and not a possible chance was left open for the claim put forward by Messrs. Hood and Corthell, and by Senator Frye, with regard to the former boards, that the investigation was superficial.

The Southern Pacific, or Port Los Angeles side of the case, was managed by Mr. Hood, assisted by Mr. Corthell. The latter detailed his theory of sand currents at San Pedro and stated the manifold advantages of Port Los Angeles, as he saw them. Mr. Hood repeated his objections to San Pedro in much the same form as he had given them to the Craighill Board and to the Senate Committee, except that on this occasion he admitted that the holding ground at San Pedro was good. Captains Pillsbury, Salmond, Johnson and Dornfield testified to the excellence of Port Los Angeles as a safe landing for ships, and Division Superintendent J. A. Muir and A. M. Jamison, of the Southern Pacific, supplied some important details for the Santa Monica side of the case. Mr. J. S. Slauson and ex-Senator Cornelius Cole were also heard on that side.

The San Pedro case was under the management of Mr. John F. Francis and Mr. Henry Hawgood, who represented the Free Harbor League, and Mr. T. E. Gibbon and

Mr. Robert Moore, who represented the Terminal. The technical side of the matter was presented by Mr. Hawgood and Mr. Moore. The navigation features were described by Captains Weldt, Polhamus, Smith and A. J. Johnson. Mr. Patterson presented the views of the League, in the form of a petition from business men representing over $15,000,000 of capital, which set forth the conviction of the signers that the commercial interests of the section would be best subserved by the selection of San Pedro, for the reason that that harbor would be "free to all railways that may desire to enter, an advantage that cannot be enjoyed at any other point now under discussion."

There is an element of grim sarcasm in the sentence with which the petition filed by Mr. Patterson closes:

"As a proof of the sincerity of our position in this matter, we desire to state that we who sign this petition have not and will not sign any petition addressed to your board, in favor of any other locality."

This observation was pointed at the compromisers.

A very complete and concise history of the controversy from the beginning was presented by Mr. Gibbon, followed by an argument in favor of the San Pedro location. He discussed, in detail, the "monopoly harbor" question, particularly with reference to the protection afforded competitors of the Southern Pacific by the section of the act which provided that the Southern Pacific must execute an agreement and file it with the Secretary of War that any railway company "may share the use of the pier now constructed at Port Los Angeles and the approaches and tracks leading thereto," and that any railway company desiring to construct a pier in Santa Monica Bay "may, for the purpose of approaching such wharf or pier and for the purpose of constructing and operating the same, cross the track or tracks, approaches and right-of-way now used by the Southern Pacific, under such regulations as may be prescribed by the Secretary of War." Mr. Gibbon's argument on this point was as follows:

So we have in this harbor a railroad company occupying a right-of-way along the whole 8000 feet of the proposed front, only half of which is subject to the law with reference to joint ownership, but all of which forms approaches to wharves which may be run out into any portion of the protected area from any part of the frontage. In addition to that, this company practically controls all of the land available for other purposes, on 2200 feet of the 4400 feet of water front, which will enjoy the maximum of protection, and such control, outside the narrow right-of-way from the tunnel to the pier, is not subject to the provision as to joint ownership. . . . . So that it is not going beyond the bare facts of the case to say that along the whole front of this harbor the Southern Pacific has, and will have, in spite of the provisions of the law, a superior right with which no other company can afford or will endeavor to compete.

Very little that was really new and that had not been covered in some manner by the Craighill Board, was introduced in the public testimony. The report of the Walker Board was filed March 1st, 1897. It is a bulky volume, containing a quantity of maps and charts and a transcript of the hearing and a number of documents that bear on the case. Among the charts are sketches of all the leading harbors of the world where artificial breakwaters have been constructed. This makes the volume [Document No. 18, 55th Congress, 1st session] one of special value.

The report of the Walker Board begins with a statement of the law under which it was appointed and a defining of the work that lies before it:

The act under which this board is appointed provides for a deep-water harbor for commerce and of refuge. Under the provisions of the law, a deep-water harbor is understood to be a harbor which can be used by vessels of the deepest draft. Merchant vessels drawing from 26 to 28 feet are now common, while steamers have been built which, when fully loaded, will draw 30 feet or even more. In view of these facts, it would seem that a deep-water harbor must be one which will safely accommodate vessels drawing at least 30 feet.

The provision that it must be harbor for commerce is understood to mean that it shall be a harbor in which vessels can load and discharge cargoes in convenient proximity to suitable facilities for storage and for interchange between land and water transportation. In many ports of the world this work is done by the aid of lighters while the ships lie at anchor, a slow and expensive method, which can no longer be considered satisfactory. A deep-water harbor for commerce should be such that the deepest ships can come alongside quays or piers, where they can lie quietly during rough weather to receive and discharge their cargoes, and where proper facilities for docking and repairs may be afforded.

The provision that it shall be a harbor of refuge is understood to mean that it shall be a harbor which all classes of vessels can enter in stress of weather, without waiting for tides, and where they can anchor in safety at all times. The depth of water in the proposed harbor of refuge must be such that the largest ships can safely ride at anchor within its limits, swinging over their own anchors without danger.

The board then presents a technical description of the two harbors, after which it says:

At neither location can a deep-water harbor that shall meet the requirements of the law be constructed within the limits of the present shore line; it can only be made by a breakwater which will furnish the necessary area of protected smooth water behind it. At Port Los Angeles this breakwater must afford protection against southwest seas and swells, the main exposure being very nearly in the direction of the heaviest swell. At San Pedro the breakwater must afford protection from southeast to southwest. As the breakwater at Port Los Angeles must be some distance outside the pier, and that at San Pedro some distance outside of the present harbor entrance, the exposure will be somewhat increased at the breakwaters, this being especially the case at San Pedro, where a portion of the breakwater must necessarily be beyond the protection of Point Fermin. So far as can be judged from the evidence placed before the board, from personal observations, and from the direction of exposure, the duties which must be performed by a breakwater at Port Los Angeles would probably be greater, and the seas which it might have to resist may be heavier, than would be the case with a breakwater at San Pedro. In view of the fact, however, that violent storms and seas are of rare occurrence at either point, it has been thought right to estimate on the same construction at each place. At either site a breakwater of lighter section than would generally be demanded is admissible.

The form and character of the desired breakwater at each point is next considered. The Board then says:

The character of the holding ground within the protected area at San Pedro is admitted by all parties to be good. It is perhaps in places a little too hard, but not enough so to form any substantial objection. As a harbor of refuge, the area behind this breakwater would seem to meet all reasonable requirements. It could be used as a harbor for commerce by building out long piers from the shore, as has been done at Port Los Angeles. To reach the same depth of water these piers would have to be about 3,000 feet longer than the Port Los Angeles pier, but one-half of the length would be in shallow water, which could be replaced by a solid embankment, the construction being no more expensive in character than that of the Southern Pacific railroad between Wilmington and San Pedro. The approaches to such piers would be practically without grade and immediately adjacent to the railway tracks now in use, as well as to the facilities of the existing inner harbor. The inner harbor, however, affords possibilities which may make the construction of such piers inexpedient. . . . . . .

In comparing the two harbors for the purpose of establishing, as between them, the best location of a deep-water harbor for commerce and of refuge, it is necessary to consider not only at which point the best harbor can be made, but at which point a harbor, when so made, will be most useful. If the location at which the best harbor can be made is also the one which will be the most useful, there can be no doubt which place should be selected. If a harbor which will meet the requirements of the law can only be made at one of the two places, that location should undoubtedly be chosen. If, however, a harbor can be constructed at each point which will meet the requirements of the law, the location at which a harbor will be the most useful is the one which should be preferred. . . . . . .

So far as direct means of exchanging traffic between land and water transportation is concerned, San Pedro affords greater advantages than Port Los Angeles. Prior to the completion of the improvements of the inner harbor, it is reasonable to assume that one suitably designed timber pier, located at a safe distance on either side of the jetty entrance and practically carried out to the 5-fathom line, would accommodate those vessels whose draft would prevent their entrance to the inner harbor. . . . .

At Port Los Angeles there is at present no room for the storage of cargoes except the coal bunkers on the pier. Warehouses can be built on piers, but they would be subject to all the risks attendant on pier construction. Land can be made for warehouse and other purposes at large expense, between the present shore and three-fathom line, or even farther out; goods to be put in warehouses so located must, however, be handled from vessels to cars which will run lengthwise on the piers and then unloaded again into the warehouses, thus requiring an extra handling. As the handling costs more than the movement, it might be best to erect such warehouses at some distance from the piers and transport the goods by rail. At San Pedro warehouses or storage yards can be provided back of the bulkhead line for the whole length of the harbor, in the most convenient possible position for landing and handling cargoes; practically this is done now in the lumber yards in the upper part of the harbor. In this respect San Pedro has decided advantages. . . . . . .

It is the English practice to have at least one and frequently several dry docks in every important port. Such facilities could be provided near the shore at Port Los Angeles between the piers, and although the ground must be made, there would probably be ample room. Much better opportunities for works of this class are afforded on the edge of Wilmington Lagoon, in positions where there will be abundant room on shore for machine shops and other accessories. In this respect San Pedro offers advantages far superior to those at Santa Monica. . . . . . .

In the matter of approaches from the land, Port Los Angeles is now connected with Los Angeles by a single line of railroad, the Southern Pacific, while a second line, the Santa Fe, terminates at Santa Monica, two miles away. There are no physical difficulties in the way of extending the Santa Fe tracks to Port Los Angeles, and there is abundant room to lay additional tracks between the bluffs and the sea. The only difficulties to be apprehended are such as would arise from the destruction of the Santa Monica beach and the interference with the vested rights of private owners and corporations. There are at present two lines of railroad from Los Angeles to San Pedro, one terminating on each side of the inner harbor. The difference in the present facilities of communication between Los Angeles and the two harbors is immaterial. The distance is slightly greater to San Pedro; the grades are a little heavier on the Santa Monica line. The present lines of communication, however, may be much less important than those which will be developed when a first-class harbor is established at one or another of these ports. . . .

ADMIRAL JOHN G. WALKER.

HON. R. C. KERENS.

GEO. B. LEIGHTON, PRESIDENT TERMINAL RAILWAY CO.

THE FINAL CONCLUSIONS.

Considered as a convenient harbor of refuge, there is little difference between the two. Either would be easily accessible from the open sea, and the comparative ease with which a ship would reach the breakwater protection at one or the other would depend chiefly upon her direction of approach when she decided to seek refuge. . . . . . .

A final summing up of the case is given in the following language:

Although the location of Port Los Angeles affords all that is needful for a satisfactory harbor of refuge, it is deficient in the facilities necessary for a harbor of commerce contemplated under the law. At San Pedro, on the other hand, a large expenditure has already been made for the improvement of the channel leading into the inner harbor and in the inner harbor itself. The series of examinations made under this Board also show that any further improvement that may be needed can readily be made, and that the possibilities for the further development of the interior harbor are equal to any demand upon it which the future can be expected to make. It is the conclusion of this Board, therefore, that the opportunity for a harbor of refuge as planned for San Pedro and the availability of both the interior harbor and the Wilmington Lagoon for improvements, and development to any extent that can now be anticipated, meet more fully the requirements of the law than the possibilities offered at Port Los Angeles.

While the physical advantages of the San Pedro location naturally lead to its selection, the advisability of that choice is materially strengthened by the consideration of the extensive improvement of its interior harbor already made, conditionally provided for or contemplated as the object of future appropriations. If the choice of the deep-water harbor site should fall to Port Los Angeles, the present statute would then authorize improvements at the San Pedro location to the amount of $392,000, under Lieut.-Col. W. H. H. Benyaurd's project of June 8th, 1894, and the same statute unqualifiedly directs the Secretary of War "at his discretion" to cause surveys and estimates to be made for further improvements at the same location, so as to secure a depth of 25 feet at mean low water in the channel and interior harbor. In the broad consideration of this question, therefore, it must be assumed that the improvement of the channel and interior harbor at San Pedro will be continued. If the expenditure of public money is to be devoted to harbor purposes in this section, its division between the two points considered will fail to secure that efficiency in results which would be attained by the same total expenditure at one of the two locations. It is the judgment of this Board that the best public policy, both in the interest of economy and for the attainment of a deep-water harbor for commerce and of refuge demands the concentration of expenditures at one point, with the corresponding cumulative excellence of results, rather than a dispersion and weakening of results by a divided expenditure at the two locations. This conclusion gains considerable force through the fact that the selection of the San Pedro site will, for the reasons stated, undoubtedly involve materially less ultimate total expenditure than is certain to be incurred by the inevitable construction and maintenance of the two harbors, if Port Los Angeles were to be selected. The preponderance of physical advantages, therefore, which leads to the selection of the San Pedro location, is in line with the requirements of the best public policy as to the matter entrusted to the decision of this Board.

Taking all these considerations together, this Board reports in favor of San Pedro as the location for a deep-water harbor for commerce and of refuge in Southern California.

This part of the report was signed by all the members of the Board except Mr. Morgan. He filed a separate minority report, two weeks later, which is to be found in the same volume with the other. Mr. Morgan's views on the harbor question, as set forth in his minority report, created no little amusement, not only among Los Angeles people, but also among engineers all over the country. He gives a list of ten reasons why, in his opinion, Santa Monica is to be preferred to San Pedro, the last two being as follows:

Because Port Los Angeles harbor has about it natural features of beauty and grandeur which, added to its excellence as a deep-water harbor for commerce and of refuge, would make it famous throughout the world.

Because the name, Port Los Angeles, comports with the city of Los Angeles, whose commercial importance mainly justifies the construction of the proposed harbor. The name San Pedro has no special significance beyond itself.

In justice to Mr. Morgan it must be stated that his eight other reasons were decidedly better than those two, whose solemn absurdity caused a local publication to offer in comparison this nonsense from "Alice."

> "The time has come", the walrus said,
>   "To talk of many things:
> Of shoes, and ships and sealing wax,
>   Of cabbages and kings;
> Of why the sea is boiling hot
>   And whether pigs have wings."

CHAPTER XVIII.

The Secretary of Delay.

THE failure of the supporters of the Santa Monica site to develop any new material before the Walker Board led to a general conviction that the report, when it should appear, would be for San Pedro, since the previous Boards had come to that decision, on substantially the same testimony. This anticipation, however, was not strong enough to blunt the edge of the keen delight that the people of Los Angeles—or at least a great majority of them—felt, when the word came, during the last days of the Cleveland administration, that the Board had reported in favor of the "Free Harbor." The Evening Express, which was still a Santa Monica paper, was the first to receive the news, and from there it was telephoned all over the city. The siren whistle which the Times blows when important news comes to the city sounded joyfully, and the members of the League, divining what had happened, came hastily together.

An impromptu celebration was organized at the Jonathan club. A band of music was summoned, banners were quickly lettered, and a procession of Leaguers marched through the principal streets of the city, gathering numbers of people as they went along. There was a great deal of cheering and handshaking and drinking of healths. The fight had been so long, and at times so hopeless, that it seemed quite incredible that it was at last over, and that the invincible railroad had for once gone down in defeat.

The Santa Monica adherents took the decision pleasantly, many of them joining in the celebration. It was expected that the railroad would grasp the opportunity to restore pleasant relations between the Los Angeles public and itself by some graceful act of recognition of the final outcome. A few words from Mr. Huntington, to the effect that the railroad accepted the decision with good feeling, and would henceforth unite with Los Angeles in the endeavor to secure appropriations for the development of San Pedro harbor, if they had come just at this time, would have put the Southern Pacific back in the position it had occupied in the estimation of the people before the contest began. But those words were not uttered, neither then nor two years later, when the beginning of the work was formally celebrated in the Free Harbor Jubilee of April, 1899. On the latter occasion the railroad refused to participate in any way in the ceremonies, and declined to make any subscription to the fund which was raised, although it was benefited to a considerable extent by an enormous passenger business between Los Angeles and San Pedro during the Jubilee. It would seem that this attitude taken by the railroad on a matter that is settled beyond question, was of doubtful wisdom from business considerations, if other grounds are not regarded. It was said, and this history would not be complete without referring to the matter, that during a great part of the contest the feeling against the Southern Pacific was so strong that many shippers were refusing to send goods over that line to points where the Santa Fe was equally available. There was nothing that resembled a boycott, but the theory prevailed that the enmity aroused by the opposition of the road to the people's will must have caused the loss of considerable revenue to that corporation. The officers of the Southern Pacific deny this, with considerable vigor, and they assert that while a feeling of resentment was noticeable in some quarters, there was never any evidence that it affected the road's business, which showed a considerable increase during the period. In the absence of definite information, which in the nature of things is not obtainable, it is perhaps just as well to accept the maxim that "there is no sentiment in business," as covering this case. If the Southern Pacific was hurt by the course it had adopted with regard to the harbor, the injury certainly never showed on the surface.

And Mr. Huntington never sent the pleasant message which some of his friends predicted would come. On the contrary, evidence presently began to accumulate that the fight was not all out of him yet. Indeed, whatever else, good or bad, is to be said of the president of the Southern Pacific, it must be admitted that he is a splendid fighter.

When the appointment of Gen. Russell A. Alger as Secretary of War was made known, the fear was immediately expressed that San Pedro might have "one more river to cross." When the contest was at its height, Gen. Alger had visited Los Angeles as a guest of the Southern Pacific, and in an interview in the Herald had declared his belief that Santa Monica and not San Pedro was the proper place for the harbor. He was known to be on very friendly terms with Mr. Huntington, and to sustain rather intimate business relations with him through his northwestern lumber interests. The Democrats, moreover, were not slow to call attention to the fact, which was known and undisputed, that Mr. Huntington had been one of the largest subscribers to the fund raised by Mr. Hanna for Mr. McKinley's campaign; and the rumor which came out from the East, that Gen. Alger's appointment had been urged on the President somewhat against his own inclination, seemed to fit in with other things, to make the San Pedro outlook very dubious. However, as it ultimately came about, President McKinley disproved this unfriendly theory by finally compelling Secretary Alger to proceed with the work.

When the report of the Walker Board was made public, the friends of San Pedro figured that as soon as specifications were drawn up—which might take two months—and advertised—which would take another two months—and a favorable bid accepted, the work would be ready to begin. The decision was rendered in March, 1897, and it was thought that work might perhaps be under way the following fall or winter, or, with the greatest delay conceivable, in a year's time. Yet it was not until the month of April, 1899, two whole years and a month from the time of the decision, that the first load of rock was dumped into the breakwater; and now, at the end of the controversy, it may be said, without the fear of sincere contradiction, that at least half of this time was deliberately wasted by Secretary Alger, in the desperate hope of throwing the issue back into Congress.

Why he pursued this course is perhaps a mystery; that he pursued it is a matter of fact.

At the beginning of President McKinley's term, Col. H. G. Otis visited Washington, and was an applicant for the position of First Assistant Secretary of War. In his desire for this place he was actuated partly, no doubt, by an ambition natural to a soldier and man of affairs, but perhaps more by a wish to assist in carrying through to completion the work at San Pedro, for which he had fought so long and so bravely. An intimate friendship of long standing with President McKinley gave him reason to hope for help from that quarter, and it was freely rendered, the President urging the appointment on the Secretary. But Secretary Alger did not desire Col. Otis as an assistant, alleging as a reason that, as California was already represented in the Cabinet, it would not do to appoint a First Assistant Secretary from the same State. He thereupon proceeded to appoint a gentleman from New York, which State was also represented in the Cabinet.

Before leaving Washington, however, Col. Otis had an interview with Secretary Alger on the subject of the harbor, and was assured that the work would be pushed as rapidly as possible.

After two months had passed, with no sound from the War Department, Ex-Congressman McLachlan interviewed the Secretary for the Evening Express, which paper, under a change of management, C. D. Willard having succeeded H. Z. Osborne, was now a San Pedro advocate, and the surprising information was elicited that the report of the Walker Board was not clear in its meaning, and that the matter must be carefully considered before proceeding further. Another month passed, and there being still no word from the War Department, Representative Barlow, who had succeeded Mr. McLachlan, called on Secretary Alger and received what he declared to be most insulting treatment. The Secretary said in effect that he did not propose to answer any more questions on the matter, and declined to state when he would advertise for bids. Congress was then sitting in extra session, wrestling with the Dingley Tariff Bill, and a meeting of the California delegation was called, and action decided upon. Senator White introduced a resolution in the Senate, asking the Secretary of War why he did not proceed with the San Pedro harbor work. The answer came in a letter which set forth several surprising reasons. These were that the improvement would certainly cost more than the Board had figured; that the act called for a harbor of commerce and of refuge, which the Secretary interpreted to mean both the outer and the inner harbors, and there was not money enough for both; that to make the outer harbor available for commerce, piers and bulkheads must be constructed, which would cost the government nearly three millions more; that to make the interior harbor of any value, it was necessary to dredge it out to 30 feet of water at low tide, whereas the report of the Board contemplated only 21 feet; and lastly, that there were a number of sunken rocks near the entrance to the harbor, which the Board, with all its investigation, had overlooked.

When this document was published a howl of mingled anger, amusement and disgust went up from the people of Southern California, who saw that they were now face to face again with the old enemy, but in a new form. The voice was the voice of Jacob, but the hand was the hand of Esau. It was very like the cool audacity of Mr. Huntington to sweep away in a few words the patient work of experts, and produce in its stead an off-hand opinion as to sunken rocks or an underestimate of cost. The reader who has examined the terms of the original act, as quoted in Chapter XVII, and the findings of the Board, will experience no difficulty in disposing of all of Secretary Alger's objections that rest on even a semblance of fact.

The answering resolution introduced by Senator White and promptly passed by the Senate, was almost contemptuous in its brevity. It instructed the Secretary to proceed without further delay to advertise for bids for the construction of a breakwater for the outside harbor at San Pedro, in accordance with the report of the Walker Board. Shortly afterward Congress adjourned, and it was supposed that the incident was closed.

But Secretary Alger was only just beginning. His scheme of systematic delay was barely in its inception. The next point raised, when he was called upon by a delegation of Los Angeles citizen, was that the Senate resolution, to be operative, should have been passed in concurrent form by the House. Of all the various excuses this was the most short-lived. He was warned that such an attitude, if persisted in, would be regarded by the Senate as a deliberate affront, for which he would be called to account in the next session.

A direct appeal on the part of the people of Southern California to President McKinley resulted in drawing a statement from the Secretary that he would leave the decision of the matter with Attorney-General McKenna. The latter officer returned a prompt and emphatic reply that there were no legal obstacles in the way of the Secretary's advertising for bids. This decision rested over a month on Secretary's Alger's desk before it was given to the public, although repeated inquiries were made of him during that time.

In this way the summer and fall of 1897 passed, and as the months slipped by the annoyance and anxiety of the people of Los Angeles grew into rage and despair. It was not enough, so it seemed, to secure the passage of a law through Congress authorizing the work; an executive officer was to be reckoned with, who deliberately nullified, by a series of trivial and trumped-up excuses, the carrying out of the law. Realizing that they were in for another long struggle, the Free Harbor League and the commercial bodies of the city began a systematic campaign against Secretary Alger, whom they endeavored to reach through influence brought to bear from all points of the compass on President McKinley. Thousands of letters and telegrams were sent out all over the country to influential men; and the newspapers that had stood by San Pedro when the case was before the Senate took up the issue in its changed form.

In the month of October Alger produced his next excuse, which was that the bill made no direct appropriation, and hence nothing could be done until Congress met again. This was in one way true, for the work on the outside or deep-water harbor being placed under the continuing contract system, it was necessary that an appropriation should be passed in some general appropriation bill of the next Congress, before any actual payments could be made to contractors. The custom followed by the War Department in such cases—with which Secretary Alger was of course familiar—is to prepare the specifications, and proceed to get bids. This process necessarily consumes some time, and, in this case, Congress would be in session long before it was over; but in case the money was not actually set aside, inasmuch as the Government had authorized the Secretary of War to go ahead and make the contract, it was well understood by everybody that there would be no difficulty in finding a contractor who was ready to prepare for the work without waiting for the final action.

When the Secretary was reminded that he was merely asked to advertise for bids, and that question of the beginning of the work should be allowed to wait for the present, he developed a new objection, which was that he had no money with which to pay for the advertisements. The answer to that came in telegrams from all the papers of Los Angeles and several in San Francisco, offering to insert the advertisements free of charge, and from the Los Angeles Chamber of Commerce, offering to pay the bill, whatever it might be. To this proposition Secretary Alger returned answer that it would not be dignified in the government to accept aid in such a matter, but that he had submitted the question of funds for advertising to the Judge Advocate General. Why he selected that functionary, whose legal duties are of a purely military character, will always remain a mystery, unless the theory which was offered at that time was correct, that he was trying one officer after another in the hope of getting a friendly decision somewhere, just as the Santa Monica advocates had formerly gone from one Board to another.

However, the Judge Advocate General decided that the $50,000 appropriated for the expense of the investigation of the harbors, a part of which remained unexpended, was available.

In the meantime Attorney General McKenna had been placed on the Supreme Bench and his place filled by John W. Griggs. Mr. Alger now proposed, with most unparalleled effrontery, to submit the matter to him, although it had already been fully covered by his predecessor in office. It was about this time that General Rosecrans, President McKinley's old commander, who was then passing his last days in Los Angeles, wrote to the President detailing at some length the nature of the outrage that was being put upon Southern California; and the result of that and of other forms of influence that had been at work was to cause the President to instruct Secretary Alger immediately to advertise for bids. These instructions were obeyed. It took some time to prepare the specifications, for none of the preliminary work had been done in all these wasted months; but on the 10th of February, 1898, almost a year after the report of the Walker Board, the bids were opened.

They were most surprisingly favorable. Out of the seventeen bids filed, only one was for an amount greater than the $2,900,000 provided by the law, thus completely disproving Secretary Alger's assertion, so often repeated, that the work could not be done for the amount appropriated. This particular bid was from a New York firm in the sum of $4,595,516, which, as it was about twice the average of the bids, and more than $3,000,000 above the lowest bid, was generally believed to be put in for some particular purpose —perhaps at Mr. Alger's request.

The lowest bid was from the Chicago contracting firm of Heldmaier & Neu, for $1,303,198. The majority of the bids were under $2,000,000.

A few days later the Sundry Civil Appropriation bill, bearing an item of $400,000, the initial appropriation for San Pedro under the continuing contract, came up in the House and a very singular incident occurred—one that has since given rise to no little speculation as to its true inwardness.

When the item was reached in the reading of the bill, Mr. Grosvenor, of Ohio, rose in the House Committee of the Whole to ask some questions. He desired to know whether the exact total cost of this improvement was known, and whether any contract had been let, and also whether it was not a fact that "a proposition had been made to make a harbor of similar character at a location in the immediate vicinity of San Pedro harbor by private enterprise—covering all the possibilities of benefit to the government to be made and turned over to the government without cost."

Mr. Cannon, of Illinois, the Chairman of the Committee on Appropriations, replied at considerable length, quoting the law of '96, which he declared to be ambiguous, and the opinion of the Attorney General, from which he was inclined to dissent. With regard to the alleged offer of Mr. Huntington to construct the harbor at Santa Monica for nothing, Mr. Cannon said that he had no official knowledge of it, but that it would not influence the Committee's decision to give the appropriation to San Pedro for the construction of the harbor in acordance with the Act of '96. Mr. Grosvenor then proposed that the matter should go over

HENRY A. COOPER, M. C., Wisconsin.

to the next day, when Mr. Henry A. Cooper, of Wisconsin, took the floor, and in very plain language demanded to know what all this meant. Was it an effort to open up the question again? He said:

> This matter of San Pedro harbor is to me in many respects the most astonishing that I have ever encountered since I have had a seat in this House. I do not believe it ever had its counterpart in the legislative history of the country. . . . . . Is it not strange that after two Boards of Engineers had said that San Pedro was the only place to improve, nevertheless, the provision was inserted in the bill of the last session for the improvement of Santa Monica at an expense of $2,900,000? Not one single member of

either branch of Congress from California wanted it, save only one man, and he is the only man who voted for the Funding Bill. Does the light begin to break? We could not get the appropriation for San Pedro. The bill went to the Senate, and after a great deal of discussion there, they finally inserted in the bill the provision for the appointment of an entirely new board—unprecedented in the history of harbors in the United States. This board, by a majority of four to one, reported in favor of confirming the decisions of the former two boards. And notwithstanding that, a persistent, unremitting, unrelenting, determined effort has been made to defeat that measure, and prevent the improvement of San Pedro harbor. Letters have been written, interviews have been had, alleged questions about the proper construction to be put upon the law have been asked, and finally the opinion of the Attorney General has been sought, and we have his decision in favor of San Pedro added to all the others. . .

Now, Mr. Chairman, if anything ought to be passed by this committee and this House—if not another provision in the bill passes this provision ought to pass. [Applause.]

It is time that people, who propose to fight, as these have, violating every precedent, who at last get a decision from the Attorney General, and then question his opinion—it is time that they should be taught a lesson that the patience of the American people on this subject has been exhausted.

No question ever presented to me since I have been a member of this House has struck me with as much astonishment as this. I have never known anything like so determined a fight to thwart the will of the people, to prevent the carrying out of just laws, in the interest of private individuals and of one corporation. And now these people, who have been defeated year in and year out in their efforts to establish a harbor at Santa Monica, come in and say: "We will build a harbor and give it to the United States, if you will put it where the engineers of the United States Army think it ought not to go."

Mr. Cooper's remarks put a stop to the discussion. The item was passed without further question. It was evident from the reception which the House gave to the Wisconsin man's utterance that that body was not inclined to consider any new propositions from Mr. Huntington, and if Mr. Grosvenor or any one else had something ready, he evidently thought best to withdraw it until a more favorable opportunity should appear.

That evening Mr. Cooper received a telegram from John F. Francis, informing him that several thousand men in Los Angeles and Southern California were drinking his health.

When the bill came up to the Senate, March 24, 1898, a proposition of an entirely new order was offered by Senator Stewart of Nevada.

If the Heldmaier & Neu bid were accepted it would apparently leave a margin of $1,600,000 unexpended.* Sen-

LIEUT. COL. W. H. H. BENYAURD.

ator Stewart, who had been a warm friend of the Santa Monica plan, saw here the opportunity to secure that improvement, and he offered an amendment that the appropriation of $400,000 be applied pro rata upon both harbors, provided the Secretary of War was able to contract with some responsible party for the construction of both at some figure within the $2,900,000. But the Senate had by this time become as completely a San Pedro body as the

---

*i. e., if the estimates of the Walker Board as to the total amount of stone necessary for the construction of the break-water were correct.

Free Harbor League itself, and the amendment was promptly voted down.

Then followed four more months of waiting. The report of the engineering authorities of the Department on the bids was filed February 28, 1898, but it was not until July 21 of that year Secretary Alger found time to approve the bid and order a contract to be drawn,* and it was not until th following spring, April of 1899, that the work actually began.

The question that the people of Los Angeles frequently ask is this: If the decision of the Board had been for Santa Monica, instead of San Pedro, would Secretary Alger have deliberately wasted two whole years on every conceivable form of excuse in getting the work started, or did he merely play his part in a well-organized but unsuccessful plot?

CHAPTER XIX.

THE SAN PEDRO JUBILEE.

WHEN the last doubt as to the actual beginning of work on San Pedro harbor had died away, it was decided to hold a celebration of a suitable character to commemorate the contest and the starting of the enterprise. The date of April 26-27, 1899, was fixed for the event, and committees were appointed from a public meeting called at the Chamber of Commerce, to undertake the work of preparation.

The presidency of the organization and the general management of the work was placed upon Mr. W. B. Cline, who had been a Director of the Chamber of Commerce and an active worker in the harbor cause. Mr. Cline's high standing as a business man, his social popularity and his experience in public enterprises gave him special fitness for the work he was to undertake. The Secretaryship was filled by Mr. George W. Parsons, an active League member and Chamber of Commerce Director, who was assisted by a very capable young man with special qualification for this class of work, Mr. D. C. McGarvin.

---

* The entire California delegation called upon the President and urged that he examine into the Secretary's behavior. That ended the delay.

The city of Los Angeles was for a number of years accustomed to hold a local celebration in the spring time, called La Fiesta, which was a perpetuation of the ancient Spanish festivals. The previous year this celebration had been abandoned on account of the Spanish war, and this year it was decided to merge it into the San Pedro affair—or to speak more exactly—to give the San Pedro celebration some Fiesta features.

The Jubilee was arranged to last through two days. On the first of these was to be a gathering at San Pedro with

W. B. CLINE.

speeches and a barbecue, and on the second a flower parade and other ceremonies in Los Angeles. As one of the features of the Jubilee, it was proposed to hold a Southwestern Commercial Congress, made up of representatives from the commercial bodies of California, Nevada, Utah,

Arizona and New Mexico, and invitations were sent out for that purpose.

Wednesday, April 26th, 1899, the formal beginning of the harbor work took place in San Pedro and was accompanied by appropriate ceremonies. About 20,000 people were carried from Los Angeles and the surrounding territory down to the ancient port. The majority of these came by the Terminal road, as the Southern Pacific had

D. C. McGARVIN.

manifested some disapproval of the celebration. The people assembled near Point Fermin, where one of the Heldmaier & Neu barges, loaded with rock, lay ready for the dumping. Word was then telegraphed to President McKinley at Washington that all was ready, and he touched an electric button in his library in the White House, whereby the machinery was set in motion to fill the air chambers of the barge, thus causing it to roll over on one side and the rock to tumble off into the water. Unfortunately, however, the mechanism of the new barge failed to work properly, and the stone had at last to be pushed off by hand with much hard labor. This was accepted as symbolic of the entire harbor undertaking. Nothing about it had come easily; it was all hard work, and but for the most tremendous individual and community exertion, it could never have been attained. After the first stone was unloaded, the speeches of the day were heard. Charles Cassatt Davis, the chairman of the occasion, read a telegram which he had just received from President McKinley, congratulating the people of Southern California on the beginning of this great commercial work.

The first place on the programme was accorded to the Governor of California, Mr. Henry T. Gage of Los Angeles, who more than thirty years before had herded sheep over the country lying between San Pedro and the city. He said:

The corner-stone of commerce of this part of the State is now auspiciously laid by the actual work of this harbor improvement for which you have so long and anxiously waited.

In this hour of your jubilee, expressive of your happiness upon the outcome of your struggle for a deep-sea harbor, it affords me the highest gratification as your fellow citizen to greet here to-day that able, honorable, independent and distinguished gentleman, Hon. Stephen M. White, and to add my tribute of respect to the ability, energy and labors which he unselfishly bestowed in our behalf, and which culminated in the selection by the national government of this splendid bay as a place for a great southern port. Senator White, an ideal public servant, was fully awake to your need for this harbor, and he therefore always readily responded to your just and earnest appeal.

Stephen M. White—whose term as United States Senator was now at an end—followed in a powerful and eloquent speech. He began as follows:

Fellow-citizens: Great military triumphs have in all ages, sometimes justly, sometimes without reason, been succeeded by elaborate displays, and long and loud applause, including the many forms through which men have exhibited their enthusiastic satisfaction—their indescribable delight. But however majestic these achievements, yet in numerous instances many of their incidents are susceptible of justification only in so far as they have been essential to promote civilization, to defend it from direct encroachment. No one fails to regret the loss of life and property which war involves, the sacrifices and sorrows thus begotten. It is for this reason that a mere whim or momentary desire for conquest cannot be the basis of rational approval, but that, as I have said, there must be something virtuous in the commencement and beneficial in the product. We are here to celebrate the commencement of a work destined to last when we and ours are gone—the benefits of which only one endowed with prophecy by divinity can for a moment attempt to enumerate. I refer to the building of the San Pedro breakwater by the government. The undertaking is certain to culminate in a harbor not only fitted for local commerce or coastwise trade, but also suited to the needs of all merchant vessels, and to our warships and those of friendly powers, plying in these waters, needing for the time being a haven where they may ride without fear. Nor is this all: The United States has made giant strides in her foreign trade.

The excess of exports over imports in 1893 was about one hundred million dollars. This was considered a most promising indication, and excited general satisfaction in mercantile circles; but the excess of exports for the twelve months ending December, 1898, was $621,260,535. The Birmingham Daily Mail of January 3, 1899, declares: "In England, we fully recognize that in America we have to compete with a country of unlimited natural resources. Nothing could be more remarkable than the statistics of the recent exports of American merchandise."

Mr. White then quoted from the report of the Craighill Board (1892) the conclusions on the need for a deep-water harbor near Los Angeles for future Oriental trade and for the increased commerce of the Southwest, that would exist when the Nicaragua canal should be finished. He continued as follows:

This monument whose corner-stone has just been laid is based on truth, it is not erected to perpetuate wrong. While conceived in labor it represents only truth, honesty and honor. It suggests the power of the people; it rises because of the people's will. The dazzling beauties of money—the allurements of millions have not obscured the vision of our engineer corps, and should not impair our sight. . . . .

When this great work is done it will again be proved that the control of the American people does not, Byron to the contrary notwithstanding, "stop with the shore," but that we move onward in those paths of conquest where the sword does not gleam and the bullet does not kill, but where the inventive and progressive American subdues by the force of his energy and the magnetism of his personality. . . . .

Fellow-citizens: In conclusion, if I have done anything to bring to fruition the great work, I have but yielded to my duty. Proud of the honors which I have received, I care more for your approval than for any official incumbency. To succeed in an ambition to be elected to high office office is, indeed, pleasant, but to receive public congratulations when authority has passed and the official is only a private citizen, amounts to more than an impartial indorsement. I would have done my duty as I saw it, had you protested. I did as I understood it, and you have commended. This ought to be enough for anyone; it is sufficient to give me a balmy pillow.

The next speaker was Senator George C. Perkins. From his remarks the following may be quoted:

It was said that this breakwater would cost the nation $3,000,000, and the contract has been let for something over one million. The residue of the $3,000,000 appropriated should now be devoted to the improvement of the inner harbor by dredging and other necessary work.

When this harbor is completed you will need machine shops, and other great enterprises, and they will come within the next twenty years, and your boys will be learning trades for the building up of a merchant marine to put an end to the burden of $200,000,000, which we are paying annually to foreign countries for transporting our merchandise and our people who are traveling about the world. These foreign countries had built up their merchant marine through the aid of subventions, subsidies and mail subsidies. Why cannot America give a few million dollars annually to create a merchant marine through similar means? The future of this country is laden with great possibilities along such lines. Twenty years ago there was no citrus fruit shipped from the State, but last year you shipped 18,065 carloads of ten tons each of citrus fruit, with other fruits to bring the total up to 57,000 carloads, besides what we consumed and what was shipped by sea, and to this can be added 20,000 carloads of wine and brandy, while millions of tons of grain are to be accounted for in the shipments from California. When the Nicaragua canal is completed there will come competition in transportation, which will insure low freight rates, and there can be no cheap freight without competition. If my colleague, Senator White, were the only attorney in this section, generous as he is, what do you suppose you would have to pay for law? The best regulator of transportation rates in the world is the little schooner plying up and down the coast. All reasonable people believe in railroads, but we believe that they should be so regulated that they shall not become monopolies. We have now two railroads entering Southern California, and within ten years we will have two more.

R. J. WATERS, M. C., Sixth District California.

Col. S. O. Houghton, the father of San Pedro harbor, followed in a brief historical sketch of the harbor and its earliest development. Col. Will A. Harris spoke of the splendid future that the construction of the harbor opened before Los Angeles. Judge James G. Maguire, who had represented a San Francisco district in Congress through all the years of the contest, and who had been of great service to the San Pedro cause, gave some of the details of the fight in the House. He was followed by Mayor James Phelan of San Francisco, who presented the greetings of the Northern metropolis. Mr. Geo. S. Patton testified to the courageous and determined work done by the entire California Congressional delegation for San Pedro, without which the victory could never have been achieved, and Col. George H. Mendell spoke of the technical and engineering side of the work. The new Congressman from the Los Angeles district, Mr. R. J. Waters, was then introduced, and in a pleasing speech promised to do all in his power to promote the continuance of the harbor improvement. Captain James J. Meyler, who was in charge of the work, made a few appropriate remarks.

Mr. T. E. Gibbon spoke of the value of the service that Mr. Maguire had rendered at the time when the bill containing the provision for the last Board was held up in conference, and Mr. T. L. Ford, the Attorney-General of the State, closed the exercises of the day with an eloquent tribute to the great physical beauty and commercial progressiveness of the Southern section of the State. A grand barbecue was then served, at which 15,000 people were fed.

The celebration of Thursday, April 27, began at the Chamber of Commerce, where several hundred of the most active San Pedro workers were gathered. A large silver loving cup was presented to C. D. Willard, who, during the greater part of the contest, was Secretary of the Chamber of Commerce, but who at this time was general manager of the Evening Express. A graceful presentation speech was made by Mr. Henry T. Hazard. The inscription on the cup read as follows:

Presented to
C. D. WILLARD
By his fellow-citizens, in token of their appreciation of his patriotic and efficient services as secretary of the Chamber of Commerce, in aiding to secure a free harbor for Los Angeles at San Pedro.
FREE HARBOR JUBILEE.
April 27, 1899.

A large crowd of people, headed by the officers of the Jubilee, then proceeded to the office of the Los Angeles Times to do that newspaper an honor which is, perhaps, unique in the history of American journalism. An English paper, the London Times, once enjoyed a similar experience. A memorial tablet of granite had been prepared some days before, and had been put in place in the wall of the Times Building, near the corner-stone, and it was now to be unveiled with appropriate ceremony. The tablet bore the following inscription.

The speech of the occasion was delivered by Mr. T. E. Gibbon, who, after a short introduction, said:

Your fellow-citizens are mindful of the fact that when this contest first began a great phalanx of wealth and power was arrayed on the side which they conceived to be opposed to their rights and privileges; an opposition so strong and relentless as to give pause to anyone thinking to meet it. They are also mindful of the fact that at that time, and without pausing to count the odds opposed, but with the desire and intent of sustaining the right and advocating the truth, as you saw it, your journal, enlisted under the banner of the people's rights, waged unflagging and relentless war against all the forces which were seeking to enthrall and entrammel the commerce of our city for all future time.

During the more than seven years which have elapsed since this contest was begun, there has never for a moment been a halt or shadow of turning in your pursuit of the path which you entered, a road at the end of which lay the fruition of a people's hopes and the vindication of a people's rights. During that time your fellow-citizens have ever looked to your columns for a defense of these rights and an expression of the arguments to sustain and enforce them, and they have never looked in vain. No sculptured or lettered stone is necessary to enable them to hold in lifelong memory the loyal and patriotic devotion which you have shown to the best interests of the community which your paper serves, but that their children and their children's children may be taught the lesson of remembrance and appreciation for services so rare in the purity of their patriotism and devotion to the public weal as they were strenuous and unflagging in their constancy and devotion, your fellow-citizens now ask permission to present to you and to install in the wall of the home of your journal the tablet which I now unveil, bearing an inscription intended to be expressive of their sentiments toward you.

Here Mr. Gibbon unveiled the tablet, and read to the crowd the inscription.

Brigadier-General Otis, the owner of the Times, was absent, in active service in the Philippines, and Mr. Harry Chandler, who in his absence served as general manager of the paper, responded in a few modest words, in which he gave due credit to the people of Los Angeles for their courage in the long fight.

On this tablet is written. "Commemorates their appreciation for services." That the paper did render services was true only because of the broad character and farsightedness of Los Angeles' leading citizens, who in this harbor fight were quick to discern the right and quick to act.

When the newspaper gave publicity to the facts of the harbor fight, showing the magnitude of the contest, and the relative merits of the contesting ports, then our citizens of intelligence gave unsparingly of their time and money to the work of opposing selfishness and corporate greed, and to exposing corporate infamy, to the end that this choice and chosen part of the world that we proudly call home might have a free harbor. Had the citizens been less patriotic, less enterprising, less generous or less discerning, the best newspaper in the world might have howled until doomsday and have performed no effective service, because without these qualities in the people the printed word would have been carried to those who, "having ears to hear, hear not, and having eyes to see, see not."

Senators White and Perkins, Judge Maguire, and the managing editor of the paper, Mr. L.E. Mosher, were called upon, and each spoke a few words.

In the afternoon of that day a superb floral parade was presented, which 100,000 people, from Los Angeles and the surrounding territory, witnessed. It was several miles in length, and contained, besides the flower decked vehicles, a remarkable display by the Chinese of Los Angeles of the ancient Oriental costumes and customs, a large company of Spanish caballeros or rough riders, the fire department and numerous uniformed organizations, chief among which was the Americus Club of Pasadena.

The floral parade was fully up to the high standard of the Fiestas and contained over 100 beautifully decorated vehicles. The Chamber of Commerce, Jonathan Club, Free Harbor League, State Normal School, Pasadena High School, Throop Polytechnic, and Los Angeles Military Academy, each appeared with a float or a coach, and the Mayor and Park Commissioners turned out a float of striking beauty. Among the individual turn-outs of special excellence were those of Griffith J. Griffith, W. B. Cline, Mrs. S. M. Bradbury, Miss Jessie Hartwell, A. W. Skinner, Mrs. D. S. Bassett, F. G. Kay, Robert McGarvin, Will Knippenberg, H. G. Rissman, Mrs. J. E. Doty, Byron Erkenbrecher, M. Esternaux, Guillermo Andrade.

A remarkable illumination that night of the business section of the city with many thousand incandescent lights closed the Free Harbor Jubilee.

CHAPTER XX.

The Present Work.

HELDMAIER & NEU, the contractors who offered the lowest bid on the harbor work, were a Chicago firm then engaged on the drainage canal and on extensive harbor and canal work in other sections of the Union. Long experience with harbor pitfalls had made the people of Los Angeles excessively wary, and they paused to look into the reputation and standing of the firm before rejoicing overmuch at the lowness of the bid. The investigation showed that the Chicago men were entirely reliable; that they were bona fide, practical contractors, and not a dummy construction company. Even Mr. Alger, after taking six long months to investigate and think it over, could find no cause for complaint. The contract was therefore finally let in the summer of 1898.

The specifications which accompany the contract call for the building of a breakwater about 8500 feet long which "may be increased, if found practicable, without exceeding an aggregate cost of $2,900,000." The depth at mean low water along the site of the work is said to vary from 24 to 52 feet. This will call for a total of 2,290,000 long tons of stone. The amount of stone would fill 92,000 cars or 3,680 trains.

The method of work is as follows: The foundation layer consists of small stones, weighing from 5 pounds up to 100 pounds, and these are spread over the bottom of the ocean, two feet thick and as wide as may be necessary to hold the general structure, whose bottom width varies with depth of the water. On this foundation lies the substructure, which consists of two parts, that below the "plane of rest," which is a plane 12 feet below mean low water and that above it. The whole substructure is to be made of stone that is hard and durable and not liable to disintegrate in sea water, and must weigh when dry at least 130 pounds to the cubic foot. No stone is to weigh less than 100 pounds, and one-third of each load must be made up of stones of over 1000 pounds each and another third of stones of over 4000 pounds each.

This stone, which forms the great body of the work, is to be dumped in from the bottom dumping barges on the foundation of rock already laid up to the plane of rest, 55 feet out from the center line of the breakwater on the sea side and 35 feet out on the harbor side. In short, at a point 12 feet below low water, the wall will be 90 feet wide. The upper section of the substructure is to be put in place when the section below the plane of rest shall have had six months for settlement. It measures at the top, which is near low water, nineteen feet on each side of the center line. This gives it, of course, a much greater slope on the sea side than on the harbor side.

The superstructure is built of huge stones weighing from 6000 to 16,000 pounds each, arranged like steps, with the heavier ones on the sea side.

Thus the breakwater, when finished, will show at low tide a flight of seven steps, with two feet risers on the harbor

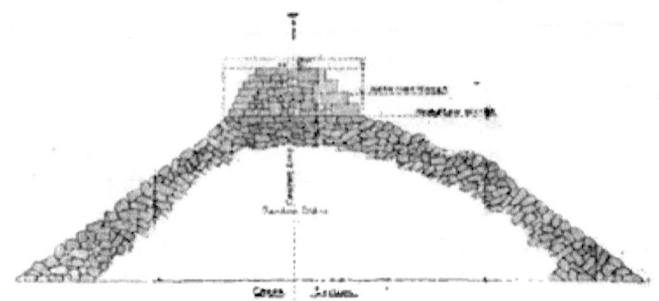

CROSS SECTION OF BREAKWATER WORK.

side, or of four steps of about four feet each on the sea side. At high tide only half of the steps will be visible. Each end of the breakwater will be formed of a single block of concrete 40 feet square and 20 feet high. [See accompanying diagram.]

All bids were made in two forms: The contractor might have stone from San Clemente if he choose, for nothing, as the government own the quarries there, or he might provide stone from private quarries at some nearer point. The Heldmaier & Neu bid asked over $300,000 more to do the work with stone from private quarries than from San Clemente; but when the Banning Bros., who own Catalina Island, and the Terminal Railway had finished bidding against each other, the contractors found the stone on Catalina Island cheaper for actual use than that on San Clemente.

In January of 1899, Mr. Peter W. Neu, the junior member of the firm, came to Los Angeles to take charge of the work, but on the 4th of February he met with an unfortunate accident in the overturning of a tally-ho, and his death ensued. Since then the work has been under the supervision of Mr. Ernest Heldmaier, with Mr. J. W. Wyckoff in charge at San Pedro, and Mr. J. S. Anunsen superintending the quarry at Catalina. The rock is obtained from a point near the Isthmus, 13 miles from Avalon.

Four barges have been thus far constructed, two of which will carry 800 tons each and two 1400 tons each. At the present time about 2600 tons of rock is placed in the breakwater every week. When the barges are all constructed they will deliver about 2500 tons per day. It will take between four and five years to finish the work.

Within two years the harbor will begin to prove serviceable, particularly for purposes of refuge. To make it valuable for commerce, a long wharf must be constructed, costing perhaps half as much as the one that now stands at Santa Monica. The Southern Pacific is not likely to build such a wharf at present, and no other corporation or individual is in a position to be sufficiently benefited to justify its immediate construction.

The commercial situation with regard to the harbor is, indeed, somewhat peculiar, and needs to be analyzed to be understood. The report of the Craighill Board, it will be remembered, called for a single curved breakwater, connecting with the shore, extending out 8200 feet into the ocean and 20 feet wide. On this it was supposed two railway tracks would be laid, and on the harbor side short piers would be constructed; and in this way ship and rail could be brought together. The excellence of this plan formed the basis of many an argument in favor of San Pedro. But the Walker Board held that it was impracticable, and gave the breakwater a different form. The result is a harbor which is, as the Walker Board says, available for commerce, but it is not immediately and conveniently available.

It was always assumed by the deep-water harbor advocates

that when the government should decide to undertake the project, it would include with the work a considerable improvement of the inner harbor. Lieut.-Col. Benyaurd had developed a plan for 18 feet of water at low tide, which would admit much of the coastwise trade. This was to cost under $400,000, and it was regarded as so eminently desirable by the members of the Free Harbor League that many of them believed it would take precedence over any consideration of an outside harbor. The reader who has followed this narrative will remember that the League asked nothing more than the interior harbor improvement at the beginning of the harbor campaign of 1896, but when it was discovered that, for some mysterious reason, there was an anxiety on the part of the River and Harbor committee and the Commerce Committee to spend $3,000,000 on Santa Monica, the whole of that sum was promptly claimed for San Pedro. In this way the work came to be done somewhat out of the natural and logical order. It is as though a community should construct an enormous bridge with its approaches so small as to make a great part of the structure useless.

The difficulty is of only a temporary character, and will be remedied either by the building of piers into the outer harbor by private enterprise or by the improvement of the inner harbor by government action.

The work which now lies before the people of Los Angeles is to secure an additional appropriation for the inside harbor work. The first step has been already taken in this direction by Senator White, who introduced in the last session of Congress a resolution instructing the engineers of the government to investigate the interior harbor of San Pedro with a view to ascertaining its possibilities for further development. A preliminary investigation has been made by Capt. J. J. Meyler, and a thorough survey will presently be undertaken. The report which in all probability will be made to the next Congress will outline several projects of varying cost from that of Lieut.-Col. Benyaurd for 18 feet, at a cost of $400,000, to that proposed by Mr. White, which involves the construction of a large and deep interior basin at a cost of over a million. From among these projects Congress will make a choice, and will continue and complete in the interior harbor the work begun by the construction of the breakwater.

The amount originally appropriated was $2,900,000, of which the Heldmaier & Neu contract calls for $1,303.198. But it must be remembered that the amount of stone required in the construction of the breakwater is not a known definite quantity, but it is estimated, with the understanding that if the amount needed goes beyond the estimate, the contractors are to furnish the remainder at the same price per ton. Thus, while we know that the breakwater will not cost less than $1,300,000, we do not know how much more than that sum it may cost. There is a tendency on the part of such works to exceed the estimates. Yet the margin in this case is so considerable—$1,600,000—that Congress is likely to take this into consideration in deciding whether the San Pedro inner harbor shall receive the appropriation necessary to make the whole project of commercial value.

In other words, having shown a willingness to spend $2,900,000 on this improvement, Congress may be expected to care very little whether it is to be spent on the outside or the inside harbor. This is an engineering detail; and yet action by Congress must be had in order to secure the money.

There is no reason to believe that the efforts of the people of Los Angeles to secure a logical and a necessary enlargement of the harbor work will meet with any further opposition from Mr. Huntington. As the government is now irretrievably committed to the San Pedro site, the main question will not be opened again, and no motive can exist for interfering with a mere detail of the general project. Such sentiments as desire for revenge or chagrin over defeat are not to be attributed to a man of Mr. Huntington's breadth and strength. As Mr. Arthur McEwen sagely observes, while corporations have no souls, they are also without the petty passions of individuals, their spite and anger and pride. It is Mr. Huntington's chief purpose in life to develop and enlarge and strengthen the various commercial interests that are under his control, and it is quite incredible that he should turn aside from the great purposes in which he is engaged wantonly to attack those who lie out of his path. This matter is referred to here, because it is a not infrequent subject of conjecture and discussion in Los Angeles among those who devoted years to the harbor contest, and who are prepared to continue with the work until their full purpose is achieved. Among these people there exists no unfriendly sentiment toward Mr. Huntington—indeed, many of them confess to a feeling of considerable admiration for him. They will admit without equivocation that the harbor is, in one sense, owed to Mr. Huntington; for it was his powerful arm that reached over the heads of all our representatives, in a year when economy in national expenditure was especially demanded, and gathered in the great sum that was needed for the work. The appropriation once allowed for a harbor near Los Angeles, the superior merit of San Pedro, backed up by a strong fight, placed the improvement where the people of Southern California believe it properly belongs. Mr. Huntington's plans were defeated; but it is not impossible for him to revise those plans to fit the new conditions. Los Angeles will become a great city, and will serve as the western gateway to an enormous commerce across the Pacific. In the development of their large mutual interests it is best for the people of Los Angeles and for the owners of the Southern Pacific that friendship and good will and unity should take the place of the warfare that has existed through a long term of years. The original cause of the difficulty, the question of the site of the deep-sea harbor, has now been removed; and it will certainly not be the fault of the intelligent business men of Los Angeles if this unfortunate breach between the railway and the people is allowed to continue and to grow wider.

APPENDIX.

The full text of the two items in the Bill of 1896 relating to San Pedro and Santa Monica is as follows:

For a deep water harbor of commerce and of refuge at Port Los Angeles in Santa Monica Bay, California, or at San Pedro, in said State, the location of said harbor to be determined by an officer of the navy, an officer of the Coast and Geodetic Survey, to be detailed by the Superintendent of said survey, and three experienced civil engineers, skilled in riparian work, to be appointed by the President, who shall constitute a Board, and who shall personally examine said harbors, the decision of a majority of which shall be final as to the location of said harbor. It shall be the duty of said Board to make plans, specifications and estimates for said improvement. Whenever said Board shall have settled the location, and made report to the Secretary of War of the same, with said plans, specifications and estimates, the Secretary of War may make contracts for the completion of the improvement of the harbor so selected by said Board, according to the project reported by them, at a cost not exceeding in the aggregate two million, nine hundred thousand dollars, and fifty thousand dollars is hereby appropriated, so much thereof as may be necessary to be used for the expenses of the Board and payment of the civil engineers for their services, the amount to be determined by the Secretary of War: Provided, however, That if the Board hereby constituted, as in this section provided, shall determine in favor of the construction of a breakwater at Port Los Angeles, no expenditure of any part of the money hereby appropriated shall be made, nor shall any contract for the construction of such breakwater be entered into, until the Southern Pacific Company or the owner or owners thereof, shall execute an agreement, and file the same with the Secretary of War, that any railroad company or any corporation engaged in the business of transportation, may share in the use of the pier now constructed at Port Los Angeles and the approaches and tracks leading thereto, situate westerly of the easterly entrance to the Santa Monica tunnel, upon such just and equitable terms as may be agreed upon between the parties, and if they fail to agree, then to be determined by the Secretary of War, and before the expenditure of the money hereby appropriated is made for the construction of a breakwater at Port Los Angeles, said Southern Pacific Company, or the owner of the tracks and approaches leading to said pier, shall execute an agreement and file the same with the Secretary of War, that any railroad or transportation company or corporation desiring to construct a wharf or pier in Santa Monica Bay may, for the purpose of approaching such wharf or pier, and for purpose of constructing and operating the same, cross the track or tracks, approaches and right of way now used by the Southern Pacific Company, under such regulations as may be prescribed by the Secretary of War, and upon the payment of such compensation as that officer may find to be reasonable Provided further, That in the event said harbor is located at Port Los Angeles, no greater royalty for the rock used in construction of the breakwater than twelve and a half cents a cubic yard shall be charged, and the Southern Pacific Company shall charge no more than half a cent a ton per mile for freight on rock transported over its road.

Improving Wilmington Harbor, California, in accordance with the project, submitted February 7th, 1895, fifty thousand dollars:

Provided, That contracts may be entered into by the Secretary of War for such materials and work as may be necessary to complete such project, to be paid for as appropriations may from time to time be made by law, not to exceed in the aggregate three hundred and forty-two thousand dollars, exclusive of the amount herein appropriated; but no such contracts shall be entered into until the Board provided for in this act to determine the location of a deep-water harbor for commerce and of refuge, as between Port Los Angeles in Santa Monica Bay and San Pedro, in the State of California, has made its report to the Secretary of War, and not at all if said report shall be in favor of San Pedro for the location of said harbor.

FREE HARBOR LEAGUE.

The roll of members of the Free Harbor League contained the following:

Allen Bros. & Co., fruit shippers, Arnott & Sumner, farm implements, Anderson & Chanslor, grocers, M. N. Avery, cashier German Savings Bank, Fred L. Alles, printer, Wm. H. Avery, attorney, Avery Staub Shoe Co., Harry E. Brook, journalist, G. B. Barham, notary public, F. W. Braun, wholesale druggist, John Bradbury, capitalist, Bradshaw Bros., real estate, B. R. Baumgardt & Co., printers and publishers, John Bloser, carpet-cleaning works, Bartlett Bros., music store, John Burr, sheriff, N. T. Ball, cigars, L. W. Blinn, lumber, R. W. Burnham, manager Dun & Co., A. C. Bilicke, Hollenbeck Hotel, Blanchard-Fitzgerald Co., musical instruments, M. A. Bronson, real estate, G. W. Burton, publisher, Barker Bros, furniture, Boston Dry Goods Co., W. S. Boerstler, lumber, C. A. Bradley, surveyor, O. T. Bassett, lumber, M. N. Conkling, attorney, George Carson, capitalist, John M. Carson, landowner, Alfred Crawford, coal, E. J. Curson, coal, K. Cohn & Co., commission merchants, Calkins & Clapp, real estate, Coulter Dry Goods Co., C. S. Compton, city engineer, D. R. Collins, jewelry, Cortelyou & Griffin, insurance, F. T. Capitain, architect, W. E. Dunn, City Attorney, William B. Dunning. manager Chicago Clothing Co., H. C. Dillon, attorney, T. L. Duane, banker, F. C. Devendorf, agent, C. E. Day, real estate, W. A. Driscoll, lumber, O. R. Dougherty, capitalist, Boaz Duncan, real estate, Fred Dorn architect, Eyraud Bros., grocers, J. G. Eagleson, men's furnishing goods, A. A. Eckstrom, wall paper, J. M. Elliott, president First National Bank, J. F. Francis, capitalist, C. Forrester, real estate, E. A. Forrester, real estate, M. N. Francis, A. J. Fleishman, banker, A. W. Francisco, county supervisor, Wm. Ferguson, livery stable, E. M. Frasee, bookkeeper, T. J. Fleming, county treasurer, J. T. Gaffey, Collector of Port,

APPENDIX.

T. E. Gibbon, attorney, Grider & Dow, real estate, G. J. Griffith, capitalist, Godfrey & Moore, druggists, George Gebhard, capitalist, Grimes & Stassforth, stationery, A. B. Greenwald, cigars, F. A. Gibson, bank cashier, J. T. Griffith, insurance, Guenther & Bernhard, restauranteurs, Goldschmidt Bros., Sunset Wine Co., Gardner & Zellner, pianos, Ganahl Lumber Co., L. W. Goden, shoes, J. M. Glass, Chief of Police, Warren Gillelen, capitalist, H. Hawgood, civil engineer, George Hines, wholesale butcher, Hayden & Lewis, wholesale saddlery, J. F. Humphreys, real estate, B. A. Holmes, broker, Harper & Reynolds Co., hardware, Hawley, King & Co., carriages, J. A. Henderson, hardware, W. A. Hartwell, City Treasurer, F. C. Howes, banker, J. M. Hale & Co., dry goods, John D. Hooker, manufacturer, E. C. Hodgman, County Recorder, C. F. Heinzman, druggist, R. M. Herron, petroleum, James W. Hellman, hardware, F. S. Hicks, banker, R. H. Howell, real estate, Phil Hirshfeld, stationery, C. A. Hooper, lumber, S. C. Hubbell, attorney, C. K. Holloway, attorney, Investor Publishing Co., H. Jevne, grocer, F. O. Johnson, proprietor Westminster Hotel, Jacoby Bros., clothiers, Johnson & Keeney Co., real estate, F. D. Jones, stationery, Johnson, Walton & Carvell, fruit shippers, Frank H. Jackson, assayer, J. M. Johnston, hardware, E. W. Jones, capitalist, F. M. Kelsey, public administrator, Robert Kern, restauranteur, Kingsley, Barnes & Neuner Co., printers and bookbinders, Kerckhoff-Cuzner Mill and Lumber Co., John Koster, restauranteur, E. F. C. Klokke, capitalist, Paul Kerkow, restauranteur, Ulrich Knock, printer, Kregelo & Breese, undertakers, J. C. Kirkpatrick, physician, William Lacy, president Puente Oil Co., Lacy Manufacturing Co., water pipe, I. L. Lowman, hatter, Charles A. Luckenbach, City Clerk, C. Laux & Co., druggists, Los Angeles Lime Co., James W. Long, bookbinder, T. J. Lockhart, real estate, L. T. Ledbetter, contractor, Los Angeles Farming and Milling Co., L. Long, merchant tailor, H. T. Lee, attorney, J. S. Moore, capitalist, F. S. Munson, councilman, Mullen, Bluett & Co., clothiers, J. R. Mathews, postmaster, H. K. Maynard, physician, Max Meyberg, crockery, F. L. Morgan, book-keeper, A. Morris, agent, E. E. McKeever, commission merchant, Marschutz & Co., opticians, John E. Murray, clerk, H. Mosgrove, cloaks, Mathews Implement Co., Lee A. McConnell, real estate, Robert McGarvin, real estate, L. Melzer, stationery, C. A. Marriner, Crescent Coal Co., A. Moss Merwin, E. R. Meserve, real estate, M. C. Marsh, contractor, A. H. Merwin, tax collector, C. C. McComas, deputy district attorney, Maeder & Priester Co., crockery, Granville McGowan, physician, A. McNally, contractor, J. R. Newberry, groceries, H. Newmark, hides and wool, Nayerth & Cass Hardware Co., H. G. Otis, editor Los Angeles Times, H. W. O'Melveny, attorney, Owl Drug Store, George W. Parsons, real estate, Milo M. Potter, hotel proprietor, Parmelee & Co., crockery, Pacific Crockery Co., Patten & Davies, lumber, R. W. Pridham, bookbinder, John E. Plater, banker, R. W. Poindexter, real estate, W. C. Patterson, banker, J. N. Priest, banker, A. E. Pomeroy, real estate, John H. T. Peck, agent, F. A. Pattee, publisher, Frank Rader, Mayor, W. R. Rowland, Puente Oil Co., F. K. Rule, Terminal Railway Co., C. T. Rosecrans, real estate, W. C. B. Richardson, L. Roeder, capitalist, J. H. Shankland, attorney, G. H. Stoll, soda water, Nathan Siegel, men's furnishing, Southern California Lumber Co., C. F. Shaffer, lumber, Sale & Co., druggists, G. L. Stearns, manager Stearns Manufacturing Co., M. P. Snyder Shoe Co., F. W. Stedham, city health officer, C. L. Strange, superintendent buildings, Security Savings Bank and Trust Co., Savings Bank Southern California, W. H. Stephens, attorney, Stewart & Naftzger, brokers, C. A. Sumner, real estate, R. B. Stephens, agent, Theo. Summerland, County Assessor, Schroeder Bros., painters, C. W. Smith, H. A. Simpson, Stephen & Hickok, agents, Salyer & Robinson, pianos, Stimson Bros., real estate, J. Stoltenberg, collector, J. R. Scott, attorney, Sanborn, Vail & Co., pictures, George Steckel, photographer, Francis J. Thomas, attorney, Thomas Bros., hardware, James F. Towell, manager Los Angeles Clearing House, F. H. Teale, City Auditor, J. H. Trout, druggist, Union Hardware and Metal Co., Union Iron Works, Union Bank of Savings, Union Oil Co. of California, Frank Van Vleck, engineer, B. F. Vogel & Co., druggists, W. D. Woolwine, banker, C. D. Willard, secretary Chamber of Commerce, Charles Wier, manager Southern California Lumber Co., W. H. Workman, capitalist, J. I. Watson, R. P. Winters, Riverside, lumber, Shirley C. Ward, attorney, H. J. Woollacott, wholesale liquors, E. T. Wright, County Surveyor, John Wigmore, wagon materials, T. S Wadsworth, real estate, S. O. Wood, architect, L. R. Winans, manager lumber company, H. C. Witmer, real estate, and 40 of the leading citizens of San Pedro, members of the San Pedro branch of the Free Harbor League.

COMMITTEES OF THE FREE HARBOR JUBILEE.

EXECUTIVE COMMITTE.

HONORARY MEMBERS.

Hon. Stephen M. White   Col. George H. Mendel.

W. B. Cline, President
T. E. Gibbon, First Vice-President
Geo. S Patton, Second Vice-President
George W. Parsons, Secretary
W. C. Patterson, Treasurer

Chas. Forman	Fred L. Baker	W. G. Nevin
John T Gaffey	Ferd K. Rule	John R Mathews
Robert F. Jones	Fred J. Smith	W. H. Workman
P. E. Hatch	A. P. Griffith	J Ross Clark
R. H. Herron	H. F. Norcross	F. J Thomas
G. W. Minter	G. J. Griffith	H. Hawgood
P M. Daniel	Kaspare Cohn	

FINANCE.

R. H. Herron, Ch'n	C. H. Toll	N. Bonfilio
M. H. Newmark	O. T. Johnson	T. J. Darmody
Alonzo E. Davis	L. W Blinn	M. Esternaux
R. H. Howell	Robert McGarvin	Abe Haas
J. R. Newberry	A W. Skinner	M. H. Flint
W. G. Kerckhoff	J. S. Slauson	

INVITATION AND RECEPTION.

G. J. Griffith, Ch'n	M. M. Potter	Homer Laughlin
Hon. Fred Eaton	F. M. Kelsey	J. A. Muir
Herman Silver	W. D. Woolwine	Eugene Germain
Dan Freeman	J O. Koepfli	

APPENDIX.

AUXILIARY FINANCE COMMITTEE.

J. D. Stewart, San Pedro
P. E. Hatch, Long Beach
Robert F. Jones, Santa Monica
M. H. Weight, Pasadena
W. H. Barnes, Ventura
Stoddard Jess, Pomona
M. J. Daniels, Riverside
Scipio Craig, Redlands
C. E. Bemis, Covina
A. P. Harwood, Ontario
H. L. Drew, San Bernardino
Smith Haile, San Bernardino
N. W. Blanchard, Santa Paula
A. P. Griffith, Azusa
Thos. R. Bard, Hueneme
G. W. Minter, Santa Ana
W. C. Fuller, Colton

FOREIGN REPRESENTATIVES.

C. White Mortimer, British Vice-Consul, Chairman
Auguste Fusenot, French Consular Agent of Los Angeles
Maximilian Esternaux, German Consular Agent
Guillermo Andrade, Mexican Consul
Victor Ponet, Belgian Vice-Consul

PUBLICITY.

L. E. Mosher, Ch'n
W. A. Spalding
C. D. Willard
Paul H. Blades
G. W. Burton

TRANSPORTATION.

W. G. Nevin, Ch'n
G. W. Luce
S. B. Hynes
F. W. Wood
W. S. Hook

MUSIC.

J. Ross Clark, Ch'n
F. W. Blanchard
A. C. Bilicke
W. A. Harris
Frank Van Vleck

DECORATIONS.

Thomas Pascoe, Ch'n
E. L. Blanchard
F. S. Munson
Jas. W. Long
A. W. Kinney
C. C. Desmond

LITERARY EXERCISES.

Chas. Forman, Ch'n
J. M. Elliott
Charles Silent
C. C. Davis
Geo. J. Denis
Capt. J. J. Meyler

BARBACUE.

Don Marco Forster, Ch'n
Simon Maier
Richard Egan
W. R. Rowland
Fred Harkness
Walter S. Moore

NAVAL DISPLAY.

John R. Mathews, Ch'n
George Gebhard
R. R. Haines
Wm. M. Van Dyke

WATER CARNIVAL.

John T. Gaffey, Ch'n
Hancock Banning
D. A. Moore
C. O. Tucker
W. H. Savage

FLORAL PARADE.

F. K. Rule, Ch'n
F. J. Thomas
W. H. Workman
F. W. King
W. R. Burke
C. E. Day
John C. Cline
C. S. Walton

CHINESE PARADE.

John Alton, Ch'n
J. D. Putnam
G. N. Nolan

NIGHT FESTIVITIES.

H. Hawgood, Ch'n
Ad. Petsch
L. F. Vetter
Ozro W. Childs
C. F. Sloane
Robert Todd
H. S. McKee
F. S. Hicks

SOUTHWESTERN COMMERCIAL CONGRESS.

T. E. Gibbon, Ch'n
J. S. Slauson
P. M. Daniel
R. L. Craig
John T. Gaffey
Robert F. Jones
P. E. Hatch
Walter A. Edwards
G. W. Minter

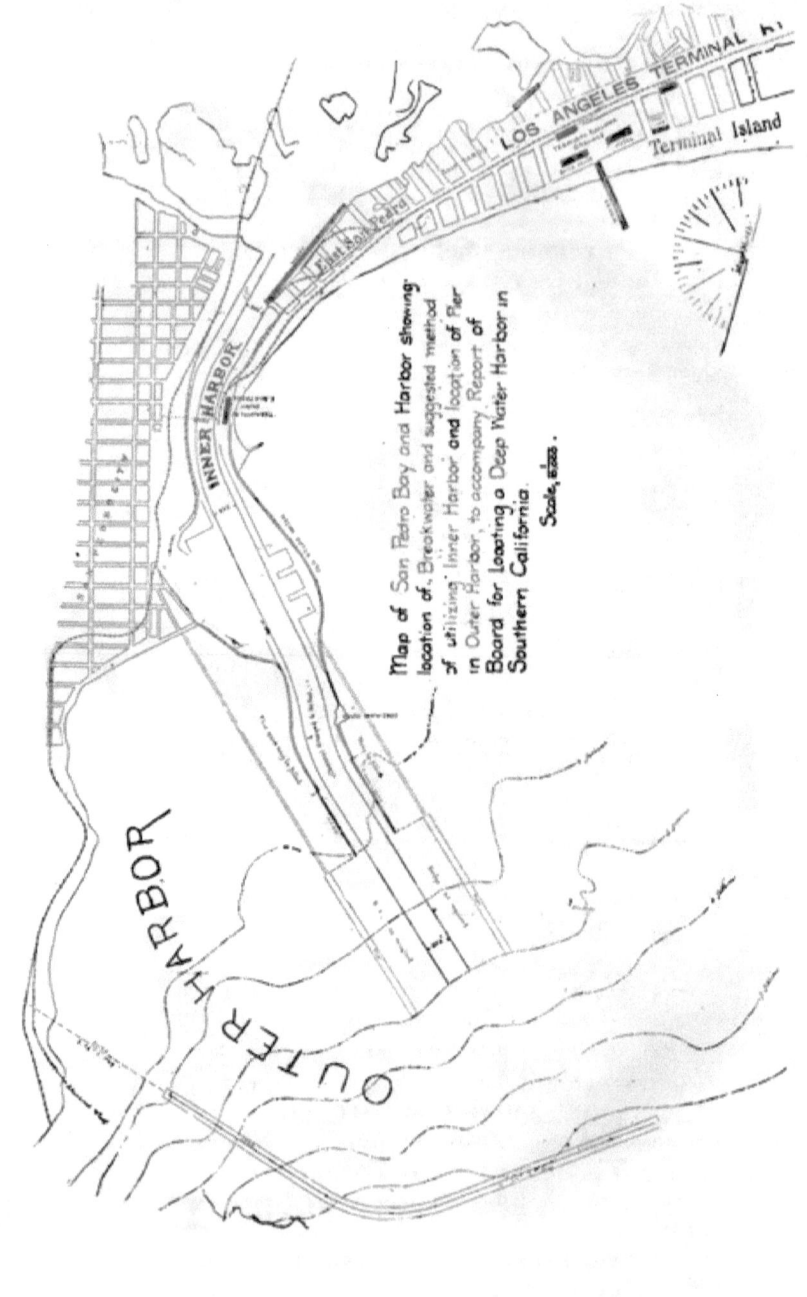

www.ingramcontent.com/pod-product-compliance
Lightning Source LLC
Chambersburg PA
CBHW020829230426
43666CB00007B/1161